FORGOTTEN RAILWAYS

The East Midlands

THE FORGOTTEN RAILWAYS SERIES
Edited by J Allan Patmore

CHILTERNS AND COTSWOLDS
R Davies and M D Grant

EAST ANGLIA
R S Joby

EAST MIDLANDS
P Howard Anderson

NORTH-EAST ENGLAND
K Hoole

NORTH AND MID WALES
Rex Christiansen

SCOTLAND
John Thomas

SOUTH-EAST ENGLAND
H P White

SOUTH WALES
J H R Page

FORGOTTEN RAILWAYS:

The East Midlands

P. HOWARD ANDERSON

David & Charles
Newton Abbot

ISBN 0 7153 6094 9

To my father, from whom I acquired my
interest in railways

First published 1973
Second impression 1979

Printed in Great Britain
by Redwood Burn Limited Trowbridge & Esher
for David & Charles (Publishers) Limited
Brunel House Newton Abbot Devon

Contents

Illustrations

PLATES

MAPS AND LINE DRAWINGS

Introduction

The so-called rush hour in most large cities is a noisy, tiring, yet inevitable aspect of daily life and one which offers little enjoyment to those involved. By 1968 Leicester was well-acquainted with the choking exhaust fumes and strained nerves characteristic of the evening exodus from the city. But a small number of homeward-bound shop and office workers turned away from the congested thoroughfares, walked down a quiet side street, through the ornamental archway of a lonely but dignified building, and along a gloomy subway where their footsteps echoed off the tiled walls. At the top of a stairway stood the bleak platforms of Leicester Central station where twenty or thirty people sat on shabby benches under the decaying iron canopy and waited for their train home. The only sounds were distant ones and even the pandemonium of motor traffic was no more than a low murmur.

Eventually, a diesel train emerged from the city skyline, lurched over the pointwork and squealed to a stand against one of the platforms. The commuters climbed into the carriages and slammed the doors behind them as millions of their predecessors had done since the turn of the century. But in 1968 this scene was about to vanish forever and the participants were preparing themselves for the chaotic business of returning home by road.

How different the situation had been some sixty years before! The nation was almost entirely dependent on rail transport then, and if those travellers of three generations ago had been able to see into the future they would almost certainly have stared unbelievingly at the tangle of cars and lorries occupying broad motorways which scythed across familiar parts of the city. They would surely have wondered, too, why the bulk of their railway system had been abandoned and allowed to sink into a series of desolate ruins.

It is the intention of this book to re-create some of the atmosphere of those railways which once served the counties of Leicestershire, Nottinghamshire and Derbyshire but have now been abandoned. Sadly, there has been ample scope for such work, for a once busy and prosperous system has shrunken to a mean shadow of its former self. In the 2,600 square miles of country, with Buxton, Retford, Rugby and Peterborough at the four corners, there were nearly 1,000 miles of railway along which passenger trains operated before or just after World War I; today the mileage stands at less than 400, of which only about three-fifths figures in the Inter-City network and seems assured of a reasonable future. An even more remarkable decline has taken place in the number of passenger stations. In 1910 there were 353 places where the public could board a train; now there are only 57 stations open to traffic, many of which are peripheral to the East Midlands area (page 13). Of the places served, only Nuneaton, Rugby, Market Harborough, Peterborough, Burton on Trent, Leicester, Loughborough, Derby, Nottingham, Grantham, Newark and Chesterfield can be sure of having a train service for some years to come. Some may express a glimmer of hope with the re-opening of Narborough station in Leicestershire and Matlock Bath and Alfreton stations in Derbyshire, but one thing is certain: the intense web of steel rails and the rich variety of train services which once seemed such a permanent part of life in the East Midlands have disappeared and will never return.

Geographically, the region can be conveniently divided

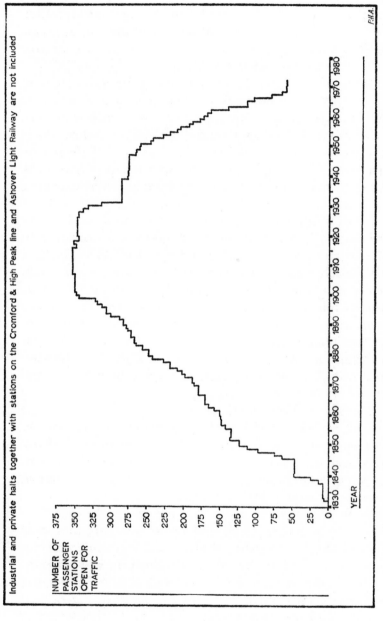

Graph showing the growth and decline of railway passenger facilities in the East Midlands

into four blocks, each of which has a particular topography, sequence of rocks and range of mineral resources that determined not only the density and purpose of the railway system built, but also the nature of the earthworks and engineering features of the lines themselves.

North of the River Trent and west of the River Derwent lies a hilly and occasionally mountainous area of limestone and grit rock where there are few large settlements even today. Some of the railways built in High Derbyshire served lead mines and limestone quarries, but most of them were conceived as through routes linking more populous areas. All of them encountered difficult terrain and were expensive projects.

North of the River Trent and east of the River Derwent the country is somewhat lower and consists of successive belts of coal measures, limestone, sandstone and clay. This is a particularly densely settled district and possessed the most intensive network of railways in the East Midlands, especially where exploitation of coal seams had stimulated the development of mining communities. Every valley had its train service; often there were two or even three lines in close proximity and dingy little stations stood adjacent to the main road or hid in the back streets of every colliery village and town.

South of the River Trent and west of the River Soar a large area of undulating clay lowland is punctuated by another outcrop of coal seams as well as the ancient rocks of Charnwood Forest. Apart from those in the industrial areas surrounding Swadlincote and Coalville, most railways west of Leicester were of a very rural nature.

South of the River Trent and east of the River Soar a landscape of rolling wolds and broad vales stretches away towards the level reaches of the Fens. Ironstone workings provided an incentive for railway development in east Leicestershire, but passenger services through this lonely countryside were totally unremunerative and many of the isolated stations stood well away from the tiny villages they served.

The East Midland countryside is rarely spectacular, yet over 29 miles of tunnelling (almost equivalent to the route mileage between Leicester and Burton on Trent) proved necessary to establish the railway system across it. It was not only topography that influenced the spread and eventual form of the network; competing interests of rival companies played an important part too. Primitive railway systems along which horses hauled waggons of coal and general goods to canal-side wharfs were well-established in such places as the Erewash valley by the time the pioneer Leicester & Swannington and Cromford & High Peak lines were opened in the early 1830s. Within ten years the routes radiating from Derby to Hampton in Arden, Rugby and Leeds had been completed and eventually these three companies amalgamated to form the Midland Railway. Over the next forty years this concern was preoccupied with building lines throughout the coalfields so as to secure valuable mineral traffic, and across country where no railways existed in order to consolidate its network and ward off undesirable advances by alien companies.

However, the Great Northern line between Peterborough and Retford began to carry trains in 1852, and by 1882 a whole series of that company's branch railways had been thrust into the eastern flank of the Midland, giving Stamford, Melton Mowbray, Leicester, Nottingham, Ilkeston and even Derby an alternative train service.

In the East Midlands the London & North Western succeeded in building only the mountainous Buxton to Ashbourne railway exclusively for its own use, yet by means of working agreements, amalgamations, jointly owned railways and running powers it established passenger services to Leicester, Loughborough and Nottingham, and its coal trains were to be seen in such places as Coalville and the Leen valley, north of Nottingham.

Finally, the Manchester, Sheffield & Lincolnshire Railway, later the Great Central, invaded the Midland territory from the north and created an extravagant new main line from Sheffield through Nottingham, Leicester and Rugby to London. Tragically, this great system, together with its associated branches, is no more and only a handful of unkempt sidings exist as a reminder of it.

As in most other parts of Britain, the Edwardian years saw train services in Leicestershire, Nottinghamshire and Derbyshire at their zenith. Sumptuous expresses pounded along the main lines of the four companies and trim local trains left trails of smoke across the limestone-walled expanses of the Derbyshire uplands, the solitary hills of east Leicestershire, the grime-encrusted pit villages along the Erewash valley, and the canal-side warehouses of inner Nottingham.

During World War 1 the railways began to feel the effect of increasing economic pressures, so a few little-used services were withdrawn, some of them permanently. When hostilities ceased the railway system was in poor shape, but the capital required to correct this state of affairs was not readily available. One outcome of this situation was the amalgamation of the old companies into four major groups on 1 January 1923. Both the Midland and LNWR became part of the London, Midland & Scottish Railway (LMS), whereas the GNR and GCR were absorbed by the London & North Eastern Railway (LNER). But the 1920s and 1930s saw few improvements in railway finances, partly because the road motor vehicle was beginning to establish itself as a serious competitor, and rationalisation policies such as that implemented by Josiah Stamp of the LMS involved the withdrawal of many passenger services in rural areas and colliery districts where buses had all the advantages.

World War II dealt a crushing blow to the ailing railway system and after nationalisation of the four big companies to form British Railways (BR) on 1 January 1948 the process of closing uneconomic stations and lines accelerated. By 1960 the increasing use of private cars had eroded passenger traffic receipts even further and the system disintegrated at an alarming rate. Within ten years almost all minor routes had vanished from the map, virtually no local stations remained on the main lines, and certain routes once used by expresses lay as derelict threads of ballast. Even large towns such as Mansfield, Ilkeston and Alfreton were denied passenger services.

The surviving East Midland lines present some interesting contrasts. At the southern edge of the area smart expresses glide along the electrified line between Euston, the North-West and Glasgow, whereas in the east the new high-speed diesel trains race from Kings Cross to Leeds, Newcastle and Edinburgh. Sheffield, Derby, Nottingham and Leicester enjoy a splendid service of diesel-hauled trains to St Pancras over former Midland main lines through the heart of the region. By comparison the remaining local services appear shabby for they are heavily subsidised by government grants and every effort has been made to economise. Seldom seen by present day travellers are the tracks retained solely for goods and coal trains which amble past decaying stations where the ticket windows have in some cases been closed for several decades.

As far as railways are concerned, the counties of Leicester-shire, Nottinghamshire and Derbyshire contain as much of historical interest, and had as great a variety of train services, structural works, station buildings and lineside scenery, as any comparable area in Britain. The motor vehicle has proved an admirably convenient means of transport for both the family and the factory-owner but it lacks the regional variety characteristic of the railway system which existed sixty years ago. By their very inflexibility the branch railway and its trains were an integral part of the district they served. Modern ideas in planning and architecture as well as nationally-based organisations tend to break down the character differences between adjacent areas, but it is still possible to examine the relics of an age of individuality, an occupation which is both rewarding and refreshing. So much has already been destroyed, yet there is plenty to see.

It must be emphasised that this volume does not attempt to deal exhaustively with every fragment of closed railway in the region, but is intended, rather, as an outline of the most interesting historical aspects and a guide to the more important physical remains of selected lines. The aim throughout has been to cater for those who wish to recapture the atmosphere of the days when railways flourished by visiting actual locations. With this in mind an extensive gazetteer is provided and this incorporates details of existing relics as well as an outline chronology of the lines concerned. Ordnance Survey map references have been used liberally (see gazetteer for details) and five plans of specific sites have been inserted in the gazetteer to illustrate just how much scope there is for archaeological research into the forgotten railways of the East Midlands.

CHAPTER 1

High Leicestershire

Cold and Lonely Hills

Though easily surpassed in height by the uplands of Derby-shire, the tract of countryside stretching away east of Leicester towards the Lincolnshire border is some of the bleakest and most remote in the Midlands. Just beyond Leicester the land-scape is one of rolling hills broken by numerous valleys where streams have carved away the soft clay, but further east a series of harder rocks form exposed summits which rise to over 700ft above sea level. The cheerless nature of these hills is even reflected in the place names: Cold Overton, Cold Newton and Bleak Hill for example. In any case there are few settlements as most arable land was enclosed to provide sheep pasture some four centuries ago and many farming ham-lets perished in the process.

When travelling through High Leicestershire one some-times catches a glimpse of a tall viaduct spanning a distant hollow or sees a sinuous trackway threading its way across the grand panorama by a seemingly endless succession of embankments and cuttings. Not so long ago the shrill whistle of a steam engine occasionally echoed round the valleys and a trail of white smoke marked the sluggish progress of a train through these lonely hills; today the decaying bridges and

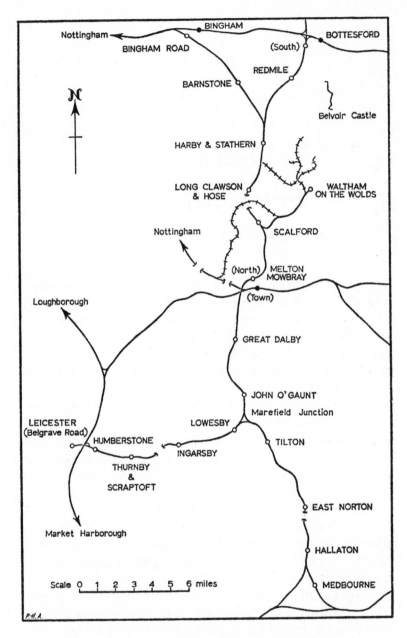

Map of the railways in High Leicestershire

overgrown formation are all that remain of the railway which served east Leicestershire.

One of the last considerations in the minds of those promoting the line from Newark to Leicester via Melton Mowbray however was to provide transport for isolated villages or solitary upland farms, and though the passenger stations were large, sometimes even grandiose, they saw precious little use. Instead, the route was a manifestation of railway politics and its disused engineering works remain as mouldering monuments to the parliamentary tussles of the 1870s.

To the north of High Leicestershire, beyond the Wreake valley, lies another stretch of upland known as the Leicestershire Wolds. Considerable fields of ironstone were known to exist in the vicinity of Waltham and in 1870 the attention of William Firth, a Great Northern Railway director, was drawn to these still undeveloped reserves. Firth, with interests in the West Riding iron industry, became particularly enthusiastic about a railway to Leicestershire and gained support from his Yorkshire colleagues in the woollen trade who bought fleece from the area, spun it into yarn and sent a quantity back to Leicester for the town's prosperous hosiery factories. As a consequence the Newark & Leicester Railway Company was formed by these individuals.

Simultaneously, however, rival schemes were being promoted by the Midland as well as the Manchester, Sheffield & Lincolnshire companies. As the GNR was a flourishing concern at this time, anxious both to extend its operations further afield and defend its territory, the King's Cross board decided to adopt the Newark & Leicester as its own enterprise on 2 December 1871. But the company had underestimated the influence of local landowners, and the House of Lords rejected all but the Newark to Melton section on the grounds that the line would interfere with fox hunting. This decision far from pleased the radicals of Leicester who held 'indignation meetings' in the city streets.

The MS & L was still desperate for its independent line to the south and rumblings of an alliance with the Midland for a joint railway encouraged the GNR to revive its plans, but in a more ambitious form. The revised scheme incorporated pro-posals for a main line between Newark and Market Har-borough to be built in partnership with the London & North Western Railway. This time the Commons were unimpressed and agreed only to an extension of the GNR line from Melton to Leicester.

In the following session a bill for the joint line was intro-duced again and this time met with no opposition. The Bottesford to Tilton section was vested in joint ownership, a spur from Stathern to Saxondale was to be constructed to give the LNWR access to Nottingham, and the curves at Marefield, Medbourne and Longville as well as the Seaton to Wansford link were sanctioned in order to provide the GNR with another route to Peterborough. Though the MS & L gained nothing from this episode, the Midland was given permission to build its Nottingham to Melton and Manton to Kettering lines.

Unfortunately for the GNR, its partner derived far more benefit from the joint line, despite having shown none of the initiative. Besides being able to run passenger trains into Nottingham the LNWR acquired a valuable share of South Yorkshire and East Midland coal traffic. For its trouble King's Cross was provided with new routes to Northampton and Peterborough, neither of which proved particularly remuner-ative. Iron ore traffic was profitable and general freight was handled in considerable quantities, especially at Leicester, but the exuberance which prompted the GNR to acquire a vast acreage for its terminal arrangements on the edge of the city seems to have been somewhat misguided. In later years the expanse of wasteland alongside the railway was a tribute to this folly.

Hunting Country

The GNR was committed to a huge expenditure on its Leices-tershire works, for the route often lay across the grain of the country and its switchback course was punctuated with tunnels, viaducts and earthworks of considerable dimensions. From Saxondale and Bottesford to Stathern Junction, engineering works were light for the rails were laid across the Vale of Belvoir, but henceforth the line climbed steadily up the escarpment of the Leicestershire Wolds. Passengers aboard trains travelling from the Grantham direction enjoyed a fine view of Belvoir Castle whose romantic silhouette dominated the wooded ridge. A half-mile tunnel pierced the hills and, after the line had emerged into a massive cutting, it used the valley cut by a minor tributary of the River Wreake to reach Melton Mowbray.

After passing through this busy little market town noted for its pork pies, the joint line headed for High Leicestershire and ascended for some four miles before reaching a large cutting at Thorpe Trussels (729128). Immediately beyond John O' Gaunt station a thirteen-arch brick viaduct carried the route across a broad valley and at Tilton the brown ironstone was exposed by a deep rock cutting (763053). For the next few miles trains passed through High Leicestershire proper and threaded the airy slopes of Whatborough Hill and Robin-a-Tiptoe. Another viaduct, this time of blue brick, took the railway to East Norton station and after a tunnel of the same name had been negotiated the long descent towards the Welland Valley began.

The Leicester branch also possessed a tunnel and a stone viaduct, both of which lay between Ingarsby and Thurnby and enabled the line from Marefield to pick its way through a particularly undulating piece of ground. Thurnby tunnel became notorious for the gigantic icicles which formed around the ventilation shafts on cold winter days, and the first train of the day often had to smash through these dangerous curtains. In fact the whole line suffered from severe weather conditions, occasionally of the kind more normally experienced only in the bleaker parts of the Pennines. On 4 February 1947 the 1.50pm train from Market Harborough to Melton Mowbray became jammed in a deep snowdrift at Great Dalby. Not only were three other locomotives marooned in an attempt to free the trapped engine and coaches but the passengers, admittedly few in number, experienced a particularly uncomfortable night.

Hunting has for centuries been a pursuit of certain inhabitants of east Leicestershire, particularly the wealthier ones, and the Belvoir, Quorn and Fernie rode the rolling pastures long before a railway was planned. It is therefore not surprising that the GNR met with considerable opposition from sporting landowners when planning their lines. The Duke of Rutland, who was the most influential of them all, was cooperative from the outset however, for it seems that the discovery of potentially valuable ironstone on the Belvoir estate had reversed his previously hostile attitude towards railways. Once the line had established itself, the hunting fraternity appeared very eager to reap the benefits it brought and special trains were often required to transport horses, hounds and their attendants. Sometimes the railway became an inconvenience to the chase and on one occasion a fatal accident happened when both fox and horse successfully passed beneath a cattle creep but the huntsman did not.

Clear indications that this was hunting country could be seen from the coach windows of a train as it climbed out of the Vale of Belvoir or crossed the hills near Tilton, for the dark patches of woodland which stood out against the paler greens of the pastures were fox coverts. Near Marefield is one such covert rejoicing in the name of John O' Gaunt (743074). In 1883 it gave its name to the station one mile to the north which had originally been Burrow and Twyford. This change of title was made at the request of local residents, but it no doubt served to flatter the hunt as well.

Respect there may have been for the aristocracy, but it was industrial traffic that earned the revenue and freight trains always dominated workings over the joint line. Ironstone quarries around Waltham were served by an intensive network of branch lines linked to the main route at Scalford, while a cable incline down the escarpment near Eastwell provided an outlet for a private narrow-gauge system. Up to four-

teen trains a day carried coal southwards from Colwick yards
to London Willesden and pick-up freights called at the remote
station yards to collect livestock, corn, beet, wool and milk.
Cattle specials ran to Melton market and the small dairy at
John O' Gaunt used to dispatch three or four tanker wagons
to London each day.

Leicester Belgrave Road handled a tremendous quantity
and variety of merchandise over the years including coal for
the gasworks, leather for the footwear trade, timber from
Boston docks, grain from East Anglia, potatoes from Lincolnshire and vegetables from the Fens. One train loaded with
farm produce ran into the buffers at Belgrave Road some time
during the early years of this century and successfully filled
part of the station with cabbages up to platform level, if
certain stories are to be believed!

Stations of Character

Certainly one of the most outstanding features of the system
was the absurdly generous provision of passenger facilities.
Not only was the opulence of the station buildings remarkable
but their very size was incongruous considering the number
of people who used them. By any standards the GNR premises
at Melton Mowbray North and Redmile were of exceptional
interest. The former was no doubt meant to be the showpiece
of the new line, containing as it did the office of the joint
superintendent. This post was abolished in 1912, from which
year control was from Nottingham (GNR) and Northampton
(LNWR) with the boundary at Melton. A contemporary account
of the station declared that it was 'a perfect model of convenience and comfort being fitted in the most elaborate and
modern style'. The report added that 'it possesses a platform
which for width, length and appearance is one of the most
imposing of its kind to be found in any of the small towns of
the Kingdom'.

The buildings themselves were made of red brick, but
lavish ornamentation in the classical style gave them a very

distinctive character. Each of the gable ends was finished with an open segmental pediment, and smaller versions of the same feature surmounted important doorways or entrances. Decorations such as scrolls, vases and garlands of flowers and leaves as well as mis-represented versions of classical columns were all used in the design with carefree abandon giving a brash and uncouth appearance to modern eyes. However, some of the Flemish-pattern carved brickwork was beautifully executed, at the eastern end of the main building for instance, where the GNR badge surmounted by the LNWR Britannia appeared within the pediment. A substantial proportion of both platforms was sheltered by gabled iron and glass canopies which were supported on cast iron columns, again treated in the classical style.

A wide subway with walls finished in vitrified white bricks passed under the tracks, and somewhat ironically its ample dimensions proved ideal for staff who occupied the long wait between passenger trains by playing football. Over its ridiculously ornate entrance on the northern platform a blue and white enamelled sign of LNER vintage ordered passengers to cross by the subway and pointed a blue fist and index finger to emphasise the point.

Eight years after it had dealt with its last passengers, the station was decaying badly. The buildings were damaged, the subway was green with damp and both platforms sported a fine display of vegetation. Nevertheless, in the peeling paintwork of one door the legend 'Refreshment Room Second Class' could still be discerned: a poignant reminder of a long-vanished era. After the site was cleared in summer, 1970, a nondescript structure housing such offices as that of the Inland Revenue was erected and local papers announced the end of a Melton eyesore. Perhaps they were right.

Twelve miles north of Melton stood the second station worthy of special note. The quiet little village of Redmile was situated amid scantily populated agricultural countryside below the Leicestershire Wolds, yet it boasted a magnificent station out of all proportion to the needs of the district. The explanation lay in the proximity of Belvoir Castle, seat of the Duke of Rutland, for it will be recalled that this particular gentleman had been well-disposed towards the GNR and to some extent the grandeur of the building was a token of the company's appreciation as well as being in honour of a visit from the Prince of Wales. The main structure was designed in the most up-to-date style and had a platform canopy similar to that at Melton. But in addition there was a tower and flag-pole, a *porte-cochère* for the Duke's carriages, and special reception rooms for the visiting aristocracy. These private appartments were lavishly furnished and included magnificent oak carvings of hunting scenes, a grand fireplace in deference to Belvoir Castle, and the family coat of arms over the door-way. During the 1940s, Redmile station served as accommodation for troops and suffered as a consequence. After its closure in 1951 the building which had seen more royal visitors than most was soon demolished (page 33).

The remaining joint line stations, though hardly as magnificent as Redmile, were of generous proportions. Without exception they stood in open country and together with their attendant railway cottages they formed a distinctive and pleasing feature of the landscape. Maybe prospective passengers viewed their location with some animosity however, for the railway was invariably a lengthy hike from the villages it purported to serve. Tilton, for instance, was a mile from its station, and the people of both Long Clawson and Hose had a two-mile trudge for their trains. The latecomers from Harby & Stathern probably experienced the most frustration for, having arrived at the railway, they had to tackle an exceptionally long driveway before reaching the bleak platforms.

All stations from Barnstone to Medbourne inclusive were basically similar in design and consisted of two platforms, each of which had a large red-brick structure containing offices and waiting rooms. A certain amount of shelter was provided by wooden canopies supported on decorative cast-iron brackets fixed to the building. However, the stations from Tilton northwards clearly displayed the GNR style of architecture, whereas

27

the remainder were unusually opulent specimens of contemporary LNWR design. Whereas the latter employed orange, red, cream and blue bricks as well as dressed stone for effect, the GNR relied on ornamental details such as ribbed brickwork, spheres and terracotta mouldings to enhance its exclusively red-brick stations. Harby & Stathern was slightly different to the others as it incorporated an extra platform to cater for connections between the Grantham and Nottingham lines, for which it was the junction (760309). The main building suffered an abrupt end to its life in the early 1950s when it was gutted by a fire, reputedly started by gypsies. A station was originally provided at Bottesford South, but passengers were so infrequent that it remained open for less than three years (798389).

A different style again was used for the rural stations constructed during 1882 for the GNR line into Leicester. Though built of the same harsh red brick they were spartan in appearance, yet the principal building had a very large canopy supported by columns. With the exception of Humberstone, where an embankment site necessitated the use of timber, all platforms on the branch were made of concrete.

But, without a doubt, the largest and best-known passenger facilities on the whole system were those at Leicester Belgrave Road (592057). This impressive terminus stood three-quarters of a mile away from the city centre and represented the triumphant entry of the GNR into another Midland Railway stronghold. Twin train sheds, each consisting of an arched roof supported on segmental iron frames springing from cast steel columns, covered the five concrete platforms. These led away from the spacious concourse which was overlooked by a grand clock adorned with a few frivolous brick decorations reminiscent of Melton North. A refreshment room lasted until the 1920s and a small bookstall closed when the Peterborough trains were withdrawn in 1916. The main building faced the road and was disappointingly plain, despite the presence of a squat tower. When the glass-roofed carriage shed was removed and a series of drainpipes were added to the walls the front

Leicester Belgrave Road station exterior

elevation became decidedly ugly. In fact the only redeeming feature was a fine pair of wrought-iron gates at the entrance to the parcels bay (page 29).

Now Belgrave Road station has gone, along with most other stations on the east Leicestershire system. Numerous railway cottages survive, but of the passenger buildings themselves only those at Hallaton, East Norton, Lowesby and Ingarsby remained in 1973. The latter, at least, seems to have a reasonable future in store, for it has been converted into a very pleasant bungalow.

Passenger Trains

As far as passenger traffic was concerned, neither the joint line nor the Leicester branch paid their way. Most customers travelled between towns which were linked by alternative services of greater frequency or convenience, and even receipts at Leicester Belgrave Road and Melton Mowbray North were pathetically meagre. Towards the end it was not uncommon for local trains to complete their journeys without having carried a single passenger.

Nevertheless, an air of optimism prevailed when the joint line opened in 1879. Every day four trains in each direction made the journey between Nottingham London Road and Market Harborough via Stathern where connections for Newark were arranged. At first the partners shared these workings equally, but during the 1880s GNR trains ceased to run to Northampton and LNWR trains stopped operating regularly to Newark. Bizarre services such as that provided by the latter company from Leamington to Scarborough were short-lived too, and with the opening of the Leicester branch a pattern of workings which was to become standard began to emerge.

The LNWR assumed responsibility for Nottingham–Melton–Market Harborough–Northampton passenger trains of which there were six each way daily, including one with a through carriage to or from London Euston. Colwick LNWR depot provided most of the motive power required for this service.

'Cauliflower' 0–6–0 tender locomotives and Webb 2–4–2 tanks were very much in evidence, but retired express engines such as the celebrated *Hardwicke* were not an unfamiliar sight in the Leicestershire hills.

It was one such train, the 1.53pm from Nottingham to Northampton, which came to grief two hundred yards north of Melton station on 25 July 1892. LNWR locomotive 1165 *Vulture*, a 'Precursor' 2–4–0 built at Crewe in 1878, had ambled along the 24 miles of track from Nottingham with its eight-coach train and was running normally down the falling gradient from Scalford when at 2.46pm it jumped the rails, lurched along for fifty yards and finally careered off the embankment taking the coaches with it. Tragically, driver Robert Heron, his fireman Henry Pollard and a newsboy who was in the train died as a result. Permanent way workers were slewing the rails, but neither had a flagman been provided to warn enginemen nor had the signalman been informed, so responsibility for the accident was placed squarely on the shoulders of a foreman platelayer.

Eventually the older locomotives were replaced by larger, but equally famous old-timers, and representatives of the LNWR 'Experiment', 'George V' and 'Prince of Wales' classes had their last fling on the line. Former Midland engines were used as well, but in 1931 several new LMS 2–6–2 tanks were introduced and considering their limited bunker capacity these machines did remarkably well on the 64-mile through journey. Despite the improved schedules thus made possible, traffic declined steadily over the years, and in 1953 there were but three trains in each direction between Melton and Market Harborough. Northampton and Nottingham were still served, but at the latter place the diversion of services from the inconvenient terminus at London Road into Victoria had come too late to have any beneficial effects. The line was ripe for closure.

The GNR based its passenger operations on Leicester Belgrave Road station where for some years there were daily departures for Grantham, Newark and Peterborough. The last of these three services was short lived however. It had commenced on 2 July 1883 with four trains in each direction, but the 50-mile route via Tilton, Medbourne, Seaton and Wansford somehow managed to avoid all settlements other than small villages and in 1916 the two surviving Peterborough trains were withdrawn as a wartime economy measure. This brought about the closure of Medbourne station, which was later burnt down, and also deprived the equally obscure GNR service to Stamford of its 'main-line' connections at Wansford. Neither of these considerations mattered a great deal though, for this particular attempt to compete with the Midland had failed.

Of the other two services from Belgrave Road, that to Grantham was the most successful. In 1904 there were five trains out of Leicester and six return workings daily as well as a modest commuter service of one train a day to and from Lowesby. The small three-road engine shed at Leicester, which survived until 11 June 1955, provided locomotives for both freight and passenger workings. In pre-grouping years these were just as interesting as those used on the joint line by the LNWR; Stirling and Ivatt single-wheelers, Ivatt Atlantics and assorted 2-4-0s, 0-4-2s and 4-4-0s have all tackled the ascent to Marefield Junction.

These were halcyon days with Sunday School outings to John O' Gaunt and hot summer afternoons spent collecting blackberries from Lowesby cutting. During market days the refreshment rooms and platforms at Melton echoed with the robust laughter of ruddy-faced farmers, whereas on bitter February evenings at Humberstone the gas lamps illuminated drifting steam as grimy workers slammed carriage doors and trudged wearily over the snow-covered platforms. This all seemed part of an unchanging scene; its permanence was taken for granted. But the rural railway had met its match and buses began to entice the villager away from his train: the long walk to bleak stations had become a thing of the past. The rolling hills remained as calm as ever, but the shrill whistle and clatter of carriage wheels assumed a forlorn air.

Bound for High Leicestershire: Plate 1 (above) *a Grantham to Leicester train poses against the sumptuous buildings of Redmile station;* Plate 2 (below) *64235 simmers under the overall roof at Belgrave Road with a Saturday lunchtime workmen's train to John O' Gaunt*

To the seaside: Plate 3 (above) *a prosperous-looking Leicester Belgrave Road at the height of the summer season;* Plate 4 (below) *the holiday spirit is very much in evidence as a Skegness excursion draws into Humberstone station on 7 August 1961*

By 1950 just two trains a day travelled the route from Leicester to Grantham, one of these being the 10.30am express which was timed to connect with the Edinburgh-bound Flying Scotsman. But from 10 September 1951 this facility was withdrawn and only the 7.35am from Melton to Leicester together with the 6.10pm return working ran on weekdays, though on Saturday there was an extra train for shoppers.

In February 1953 BR announced its intention to withdraw all passenger services from the former GNR and LNWR lines in east Leicestershire, for stations such as Tilton averaged less than two passengers a day, only 67 people used the trains regularly, and money was being lost at the rate of £29,000 per annum. Local authorities suddenly became aware of their railway. In April 1953 Billesden Rural Council insisted that agricultural communities were dependent on the line and its closure would mean a drift of farmworkers back to the towns. In any case a pay-as-you-enter, tram-like vehicle operating on a circular route via Nottingham and Leicester using reinstated connections at Forest Road and Marefield would solve all financial problems!

But vague hopes were not enough and the trains stopped running. On 5 December 1953 an ancient LNWR 2–4–2 tank 46666 pulled the last train from Market Harborough to Melton. It was an historic occasion, for though the vintage engine was assisted by a newer locomotive and the carriages were fairly modern vehicles rather than non-corridor, six-wheel 'bumpers', the train evoked memories of the heyday of the joint line. Flashbulbs popped, wreaths were laid and elderly council members bemoaned the passing of an era.

But representations concerning the plight of workpeople did have some effect, for two unadvertised services, each of one return working a day, continued to operate from Leicester to John O' Gaunt and from Market Harborough to East Norton. For the young lads who spent their school holidays at Leicester Forest Road crossing (604056) a welcome relief to the endless procession of trains on the Midland main line came when a bell rang in the GNR signal box and the crossing gates clattered across the road for the evening departure to High Leicestershire. Farthings and lollipop sticks were ceremoniously placed on the rails, the adventurous souls scampered up the old footbridge and everyone peered at the distant plume of smoke. Soon the old GNR 0–6–0 burst from beneath the Midland overbridge with a couple of red and cream carriages. The tang of soot, steam and hot oil filled the air as first the driving wheels ground over the crossing then the coaches beat out a metallic drumming over the rail joints. A few lined faces, each half-covered by a cloth cap, glanced through the grimy windows at the scruffy urchins standing on the gates, and the train disappeared up the bank to Humberstone (page 33).

To the Seaside

It was most appropriate that both the first and last public passenger trains from Belgrave Road were bound for the Lincolnshire coast. On 2 October 1882 an excursion left Leicester for Skegness and for the next eighty years the terminus was known to many thousands of Leicester holidaymakers as the station for the sea. Though insignificant when compared with the amount of traffic to Skegness, Mablethorpe and Sutton on Sea, other special workings over the east Leicestershire lines were not without interest. Waltham Fair and Croxton Park race meetings saw passenger coaches being drawn over the Waltham mineral line, agricultural specials ran to East Anglia, and trains even ran to the annual Hallaton bottle-kicking contest.

Small and ageing engines did remarkably fine work on the heavy seaside trains, often with inferior coal. GNR 0–6–0s eventually became the mainstay of these specials and many hauled fourteen fully-laden bogie carriages up the long drag to Marefield. Improvements came when it was almost too late, and in the last few years of the service powerful LNER B1 4–6–0s capably handled rakes of proper main-line carriages. The days of non-corridor stock had passed. Seaside buckets were purchased by trippers for building sandcastles alone; previously they had proved very useful for other purposes during the journey and guards knew it was unwise to lean out of their compartment windows too often!

Though the trains stopped in 1962, recollections of the start of a week at the coast will remain for some years to come. The booking hall floor at Belgrave Road rumbled beneath surging throngs of happy holidaymakers and the shouts of young voices echoed round the cavernous station. Out in the morning sunshine two grimy engines gathered a full head of steam for their respective departures to Skegness and Mablethorpe. Even during the final years there were plenty of passengers; in 1959 for example over 20,000 people travelled in 72 trains to the two resorts.

A flag waved, a whistle shrieked and the 8.25am to Skegness began its 160-minute journey towards the North Sea. The engine blasted under Catherine Street bridge, which still displayed its scrape marks from the days when tenders had to be piled high with coal, past the timber yards, over Forest Road crossing and out through suburban Leicester where more passengers were picked up. Ahead lay a youngster's paradise: sandcastles and slot machines; donkey rides and dodgems; candyfloss and ice cream (page 34).

But the time passed too quickly and very soon the train home eased gently out of the shimmering heat of a Saturday afternoon into the cool gloom of Belgrave Road station. The slumbering terminus became alive once again as three hundred sun-tanned beings engulfed the ticket barrier. The driver in a rakish cap and his fireman with a knotted handkerchief for headgear, beamed down from their cab, obviously very content with their work. Many passengers expressed gratitude for a job well done. Blue smoke and glowing sparks flew up towards the blackened train-shed roof as one small boy was lifted on to the footplate where he gazed open-mouthed at the crackling flames in the firebox and the wisps of steam escaping from a maze of pipes, wheels and gauges.

But these things are only memories. No one sets out on cloudless summer mornings with sandwiches and spades to travel the old way to the coast any more. The grandiose terminus fell silent and began to moulder; walls turned green, plaster fell from the ceilings and the rooms became dank and musty. A scrap dealer eventually acquired the structure and the buildings became mauled and burnt before they were finally knocked to pieces in 1972. A giant roundabout now occupies the site. No doubt such municipal motorways are heralded as great improvements by most citizens and welcomed with the same enthusiasm that greeted the arrival of the Great Northern Railway in 1882. There are certainly a few people, however, who feel that the new road system lacks something of the character and atmosphere of Leicester's station for the sea.

CHAPTER 2

West of Leicester

The Pioneers

Until 1964 it was possible to board a diesel multiple-unit at Leicester London Road station for the 31-mile journey to Burton on Trent. Though far from scenic, the route taken by these trains formed the backbone of a fascinating network of railways built largely to tap the coalfields of Leicestershire and South Derbyshire. Today this system is almost completely dismantled and the passenger services which operated over some eighty miles of track have passed into oblivion.

Apart from a couple of horse-operated waggonways, the earliest line was the famous Leicester & Swannington which saw the first steam locomotives in the Midlands and later formed the basis of the Burton route. When the Bell Hotel in Leicester's Humberstone Gate was demolished in 1970 the birthplace of this ancient line disappeared, for it was here on 12 February 1829 that a meeting of colliery owners and local traders decided to build a railway from Swannington to the city. Canal-borne Nottinghamshire coal was selling more cheaply in Leicester than that hauled by cart from local pits, so William Stenson, part owner of Long Lane pit near Whitwick, wrote to John Ellis, a wealthy and influential Leicester Quaker:

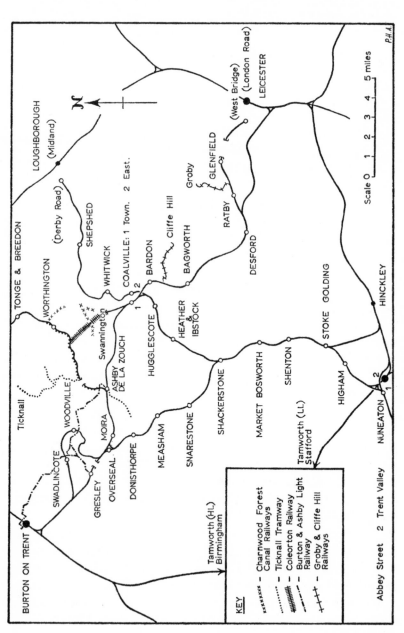

Map of the railways west of Leicester

KEY

xxxxxx – Charnwood Forest Railways

.... – Ticknall Tramway

▦▦▦ – Coleorton Railway

–·–·– – Burton & Ashby Light Railway

++++ – Groby & Cliffe Hill Railways

1 Abbey Street   2 Trent Valley

Scale 0 1 2 3 4 5 miles

P.H.A.

Our carting beats us, but I see a way of relief if we can but get up a railway company. I've tried the ground with my theodolite and find no difficulty in making, though a tunnel will have to be made through the hill at Glenfield and further there will have to be a severe incline near to Bagworth.

Ellis was impressed and succeeded in gaining the interest of the great George Stephenson with whose backing capital was obtained and an Act of Parliament secured. Stephenson's son Robert was appointed engineer and the little railway was built. On 17 July 1832, pealing church bells, cannon-fire and a feast with ale, wine and champagne celebrated the start of its lengthy career as the locomotive *Comet*, which had been brought from Newcastle by sea and canal, hauled the first train. Ten locomotives worked on the L & S during its independent existence, but they were undersized and until the Midland purchased the local line and began working it on 1 January 1847 the motive power could hardly cope with what became a heavy traffic in coal.

For the city terminus of the L & S, a site alongside the River Soar at West Bridge was selected as the flat water meadows provided ample space for extensive sidings and coal wharves (579045). At present this area is the neglected back yard of Leicester where ornate Georgian mills cast reflections in the stagnant canal and a forest of factory chimneys forms the skyline. Nearby the massive grey girders of part of the expensive Great Central viaduct stride confidently across the waterway. Here, in juxtaposition, were two railways utterly different in scope and ambition yet, ironically, the local line remained in use for almost twice as long as the express route to London.

The L & S was built to carry coal and, though a couple of proper carriages were eventually built in the West Bridge workshops, the management regarded passengers with very little enthusiasm. Accommodation usually consisted of coal wagons, with or without their contents, as a newspaper complaint of 1833 illustrates:

On August 5th a large party engaged a carriage to convey them to Bardon Hill. On their return they found it full and had to get on the coals to find their way to Leicester, where the ladies in their wet silks and white dresses (it was raining fast) cut a laughable figure. It is time the attention of the directors was called to the many complaints and not allow so many masters to officiate at the station house.

Station facilities were just as indifferent. Local inns and tiny cabins served as booking offices along the line and at West Bridge, where carriages were drawn into a siding by horses once they had been detached from the goods wagons, over forty years elapsed before a platform was provided. The 'passenger by coal train' arrangement survived until 1887 when a proper branch train of six-wheel carriages hauled by a Midland 0-6-0 tender locomotive was introduced. Following this development, it was decided to build a completely new station at West Bridge to replace the ramshackle affair by the canal towpath. These new arrangements took effect from 13 March 1893 and the purpose-built brick buildings, which included waiting rooms, a hitherto unknown luxury, proved far more convenient than the old structure. This became mess rooms for coal workers, a purpose for which it was admirably suited (page 51).

Despite these improvements, passengers were scarce at West Bridge, largely because through trains to Coalville and Burton commenced at the main Midland station in Leicester and the branch satisfied purely local needs. Occasionally its platforms throbbed with youngsters on a Sunday school treat to Ratby and in 1876 over 600 people travelled by two specials when the foundation stone for Glenfield's new Methodist church was laid. But when Desford to West Bridge trains ceased in 1928 a newspaper remarked: 'One thing to be noted in connection with the latest Leicester & Swannington development is that the public will not be seriously inconvenienced by the deprivation of a passenger service' (page 56).

So the branch settled down for forty leisurely years conveying coal from Leicestershire pits to the West Bridge wharves. At first the Midland provided a small 0–6–0 side tank to shunt these sidings, and Tom Hayward, its regular driver, used to greet fellow staff with 'Ora Pro Nobis' which, when translated from Latin, means 'Pray for us'. This, it seems, was a most appropriate salute, for in 1926 the shunt engine ceased to be based at West Bridge and its shed was subsequently demolished!

An interesting branch was that to Soar Lane (580049). It opened on 4 October 1834 to provide access to extra wharf space required for coal dispatched by canal, and was worked by horses because it involved some acute curves as well as a fragile bridge over the Leicester Navigation. As the rails hardly cleared the towpath, Robert Stephenson designed a timber lift bridge to allow narrow-boats sufficient headroom. Though a replacement was installed in 1845, the original design was perpetuated and the structure preserved by the Leicester Museum of Technology still contains parts manufactured in the West Bridge workshops.

Beyond the coal yards a single track climbed out of the Soar Valley leaving the city sprawled below. Ahead lay the formidable ridge of sand and clay which necessitated Glenfield tunnel, a perfectly straight and level bore of 1,796 yards. Its construction was a mammoth task for those days and was made worse by the unforeseen difficulties which occurred. Inexperienced contractors went bankrupt; one man was killed when he fell down a working shaft; some mortarwork was found to be unsatisfactory and extra brick lining was required through patches of loose sand.

Work was eventually completed at an inflated cost but to the limited dimensions deemed adequate for trains in those early years. Even at its opening, considerable embarrassment was caused when *Comet's* chimney struck the roof and showered soot over the guests and officials on the inaugural run. An unscheduled halt was called so that they could make themselves presentable with a hasty wash in Glenfield Brook! In open wagons the journey through those narrow confines must have been alarming and even when proper carriages were used the droplights were barred to prevent decapitations. The old Midland Johnson 0–6–0 engines from Coalville shed just managed to squeeze through, but two BR standard 2–6–0s which replaced them in 1964 had to have their cabs trimmed. In 1931 an engine was derailed at West Bridge and, as no crane of sufficient power could pass through the tunnel, it was feared at first that it might have to be cut up.

Glenfield tunnel seems to have held a strange fascination for local residents. Even before it opened, gates were fixed at the western end to thwart would-be explorers and during its last years youngsters from the nearby housing estate often became trapped as coal trains trundled through. Perhaps this curiosity is understandable, for a constant reminder of the tunnel were the eleven ventilation shafts whose brick cylindrical tops, each capped by a metal grille, marched across Glenfield Hill. Today these disused chimneys lurk between the houses on a new estate and five of them are actually in private gardens, respectably clad with ivy or disguised by new brickwork. But the days when washday had to be carefully timetabled to avoid the smuts from the West Bridge goods deep below are past. In 1969 the derelict tunnel was bought by Leicester Corporation for £5 and suggestions as to what to do with it included a mushroom farm and a discotheque. Eventually it was sealed to prevent rubbish being dumped inside and burnt, so an historic piece of engineering met a most ungracious end.

The line to West Bridge became much reduced in importance from 27 March 1848 when the Midland link between Leicester (Campbell Street) and Burton opened, using the existing L & S right of way from Desford to Coalville. But near Bagworth a deviation was built and over two miles of the original line completely closed because it included an incline of 1 in 29. The route of this abandoned railway is particularly worthy of inspection as it retains more than anywhere else the atmosphere of Robert Stephenson's line. Near Bagworth and

Ellistown station a rough lane flanked by bungalows represents the original trackbed (446091). Overlooking the falling incline gradient at the end of this road lies a small cottage reminiscent of the first Glenfield station which was modelled on the bow-fronted toll houses then familiar on turnpike roads. It was built to accommodate the contractor who operated the incline on behalf of the L & S and though recently veneered in stucco this precious relic is substantially the building erected in 1832.

The incline itself falls away as a grassy footpath between hawthorn hedges, its even gradient now warped by subsidence. Once it resounded with the lumbering passage of coal wagons and sometimes witnessed more than its quota of activity when runaways were wrecked at the bottom. In 1844 a passenger carriage met this fate, but no casualties ensued as the public walked this section of their journey. Responsibility for these accidents lay largely with the method of operation whereby one end of a cable which passed round a horizontal pulley at the summit was attached to the loaded wagons and, as these descended, the other end raised the empties. Obviously such a time consuming and hazardous operation was unsatisfactory on so busy a railway.

Half a mile south of the incline, where L & S metals crossed Thornton Lane, an inn known as the Stag and Castle once issued railway tickets. Though abandoned as a halt in 1841, the building still survives and a cinder path in front of it marks the former trackbed (458081). It was here that a collision involving L & S locomotive *Samson* and a farm cart was supposed to have taken place. One can imagine the irate rustic, face purple with rage, standing amid his scattered eggs and beetroot and gesticulating at the remains of his waggon clinging to the engine. Unfortunately there is little evidence to support this particular story, though in the youthful days of railways such incidents were not uncommon. It has been suggested that this event led to steam whistles being fitted to locomotives.

At Mantle Lane, beyond Coalville, the Burton line diverged

from what was once the western extremity of L & S metals (423148). In order to reach the heart of the coalfield at Swannington village an incline which descended for almost half a mile at 1 in 17 proved necessary. Above all else it was this feature which made the railway famous. As loaded coal wagons had to be drawn up the gradient a stationary steam engine was installed at the summit. It was built by the Horsley Coal and Iron Company of West Bromwich to the specifications of Robert Stephenson and had one horizontal cylinder of $18\frac{1}{4}$in bore with a piston of 42in stroke. This ancient machine can still be examined in York Museum where it was removed for preservation in 1952, though the engine room and boiler house, whose tall chimney was a landmark for miles around, have completely disappeared.

The engine had a less strenuous life than had been anticipated for the old pits around Pegg's Green soon became worked out and new mines were sunk further south. Califat, California and Calcutta collieries had all been abandoned by 1892. This should have meant the end of Swannington incline, but a large pumping engine to keep the underground workings of adjacent collieries free of water was installed at Calcutta shaft, and wagons of coal for its boilers were lowered down the slope. This reversed role continued until 1947 when the pumps became electrically operated and the engine finally retired.

Because of the steeply sloping ground, the upper half of Swannington incline ran through a deep sandstone cutting whereas the lower part was carried on a substantial embankment. Between these earthworks lay an elegant sandstone overbridge from which a landscape moulded by the earlier colliery workings can be enjoyed. Smallholdings and rows of cottages once associated with the little pits are scattered across the fields, while overgrown mounds marking former shale tips are just discernible in the valley bottoms.

Not detectable from this distance, however, are the traces of ancient waggonways which attempted to tap the collieries long before the L & S arrived. Sometimes a low bank between some cottages or a marshy hollow in a field marks the route, but often the only clue is a subtle change of soil colour across ploughed land. Approximately two miles of horse-operated railway opened during 1794 from Coleorton Pits to the Charnwood Forest canal which was in turn linked with Loughborough by another line from Nanpantan. But when Blackbrook canal reservoir burst during the 1798 thaw, the whole cumbersome system was abandoned and the Leicester-shire coalfield plunged into a depression ended only by the building of the Swannington line 35 years later.

A much more successful system was that opened from 1802 onwards to feed the Ashby-de-la-Zouch canal. Eventually, almost eighteen miles of plateway (where the rails rather than wheels had flanges) carried limestone and lime from the Tick-nall area to Willesley Basin (331139). As the last section was abandoned as recently as 1916 there are several remains still to be seen, including a bridge in Ticknall village and two tunnels near Calke Park. In the rolling country south of Tick-nall the route can easily be traced and numerous stone blocks to which the rails were fastened remain in situ.

During 1833 a third horse-operated line was built to link Sir George Beaumont's collieries with the Leicester & Swan-nington. The Coleorton Railway was closed in 1872 but its massive earthworks remain and at Woolroom some of the original rails still cross a lane (409178). Of two tunnels on the line, that near Newbold School remains in good condition for when New Lount Colliery was sunk in 1925 access to it was provided by a branch laid on the abandoned Coleorton forma-tion. This saw steam locomotives until the pit closed in 1968.

Railways to Ashby

When the Midland acquired the Ashby Canal in 1846 it inherited the Ticknall tramway and eventually decided to rebuild the section between Breedon and Ashby as a standard-gauge railway. The new works formed a useful extension of the existing Peartree to Breedon goods branch and on 1

January 1874 a passenger service from Ashby to Derby was inaugurated. At the former station, trains were accommodated at a modest branch platform which was some distance from the monumental main-line buildings. The line curved sharply northwards through the old market town and betrayed its tramway ancestry by the way it crept along narrow passages between garden walls and crossed several streets on the level. Some of the ancient formation was too erratic to follow, however, and a deviation proved essential. One section of the old route was retained as a factory branch and crossed the Callis by a graceful stone bridge with curved abutments in typical canal fashion (355170).

Old Parks tunnel, by which the tramway pierced a ridge of land beyond Ashby, was of course rebored to take full-sized trains. Near its northern portal, where the rails emerged in a bleak cutting, stood a low wharf serving as an exchange point for lime and farm produce brought along the Ticknall branch. This remote place was once very busy for until the line was rebuilt it functioned as the focal point of the tramway system and boasted both a weighbridge and a tunnel house. Beyond this point the Ashby to Derby line descended through Lount Woods, past the colliery sidings and on to Breedon. Once again the twists and turns of the track were largely attributable to William Jessop who planned the original course of the tramway.

The stations between Ashby and Derby were spartan affairs, no doubt to match the meagre passenger service which survived only until 1930. All of them were simple structures featuring roundheaded windows, but some had timber walls, as at Chellaston where the building still survives, whereas others were made of brick. At Breedon one of the more substantial type has been drastically altered and extended to form a dwelling. Though thousands of trains have arrived, departed and been forgotten, Breedon church still overlooks the village station from its limestone knoll and has remained virtually unchanged for seven centuries.

About ten miles south of Breedon lies Shackerstone, a tiny

48

farming village set deep in the rolling pastureland of West Leicestershire. At the end of a pot-holed lane alongside the old Ashby canal the village station hid in a serene setting of foliage and reflections (379066). But, rather than an un-distinguished halt, the visitor discovered a grand structure embellished with ornate iron and solemn stone. After years of neglect this extravagant building lay forlorn and decaying, with only the clatter of an occasional freight train to disturb its dank waiting rooms. From the brick footbridge, itself far from plain, the same visitor might have wondered what prompted the Midland and London & North Western com-panies to provide such elaborate accommodation in so sylvan a setting. But the weed-choked platforms once witnessed forty passenger trains a day and though most of them terminated locally at Ashby, Nuneaton or Loughborough some carried through coaches to London Euston.

In 1760 a rich Birmingham ironmaster built a great house set in its own deer park on gently sloping land overlooking the River Sence. Once the railway opened, guests at Gopsall Hall were able to arrive by train and among those who momentar-ily graced Shackerstone's platforms were Queen Alexandra, Princess Victoria and, on one special occasion, King Edward VII. It is rumoured that when the royal train arrived a section of platform, which had been raised so as to cause his majesty the minimum of inconvenience when leaving his carriage, in fact prevented the door from being opened at all. To the monarch's annoyance the train had to be drawn forward before he could alight.

However, the promoters of the Ashby & Nuneaton Joint line had in mind something far more remunerative than either regal visitors or village farmers. During the 1860s Euston had been casting covetous eyes on the Leicestershire coalfield which had been monopolised by the Midland. With the South Leicestershire line between Nuneaton and Wigston (com-pleted in 1864) as a foothold, the LNWR proposed the 'Coal-fields Railway' which was to run from Ashby, through Market Bosworth, to the Trent Valley main line at Nuneaton. The

Midland had already obtained powers for an identical line in 1846 but these were allowed to lapse with the purchase of the Leicester & Swannington which, together with the Burton extension, created the desired outlet for coal. Faced with this LNWR initiative, Derby revived its own plans. Eventually these opposing schemes were resolved by the creation of a joint committee and work began on building railways from Nuneaton and Hinckley to Ashby and Coalville.

Some of the route closely followed the Ashby canal, but whereas the latter twisted with the contours to maintain its level, numerous cuttings and embankments carried the railway in a more direct line. These caused considerable difficulty during construction as the contractors frequently encountered waterlogged sand and unstable clay which oozed out in sticky landslides. No spectacular engineering works proved necessary but in such an intensively farmed district nearly a hundred red brick bridges were required to carry country lanes, or as occupation crossings where property had been severed. On 16 August 1873, when the line was almost finished, a 'treat' for the navvies was held near Market Bosworth. After the train bringing guests had wound its way from Nuneaton with a brass band entertaining passengers from the last wagon, the feasting and drinking began. This was followed by an afternoon of athletic sports designed, no doubt, to counter the effects of the earlier gastronomic indulgence.

Though coal was its lifeblood, the A & N ran within sight of colliery winding gear only where its northern extremities passed through Donisthorpe and Hugglescote. South of these dreary mining townships lies a quiet pastoral landscape of considerable beauty where brick Georgian farmhouses are scattered through the fields, distant church spires pinpoint the villages and numerous spinneys clothe the gentle undulations. Such is the landscape where railway and canal curve gently towards Shackerstone (374071). An ambling passenger train of ancient carriages hauled by a black LNWR 2-4-2 tank engine seemed far more appropriate here than any coal train.

One part of the joint line which saw neither passenger nor

West of Leicester: Plate 5 (above) *a passenger train composed of six-wheel carriages at Leicester West Bridge in Midland Railway days;* Plate 6 (below) *industrial Woodville from a Leicester to Crewe excursion on 10 August 1960*

Time to spare: **Plate 7** (above) *67389 waits at Stamford East with an Essendine train;* **Plate 8** (below) *an ex-M&GNR Johnson 4–4–0 pauses at Edmondthorpe & Wymondham with a stopping train from the Fens during 1937*

coal trains was the section between Stoke Golding and Hinck-ley. Though it was completed, this ill-conceived link to the South Leicestershire line served no practical purpose once reciprocal traffic agreements between the owning partners had been agreed and it was dismantled in about 1900, still unused. Now much of the trackbed is a mass of brambles and near Hinckley has been completely obliterated. Of the three badly decaying brick bridges which still span it, one has at least found useful employment as a cow shed.

Lavish expenditure was not limited to unnecessary lines, as the ornate station buildings were more than adequate for the agricultural hamlets and pit villages which they served. Of those remaining, Measham and Market Bosworth are identi-cal to that at Shackerstone whose solemn appearance clearly reflects contemporary LNWR policy. The structure at Stoke Golding, though basically similar in size and shape, displays the polychrome Gothic more characteristic of Midland archi-tecture. Passenger services, which began on 1 September 1873, were worked by both partners. Midland trains operated from Ashby to Nuneaton (Abbey Street) and from Coalville to Market Bosworth, whereas LNWR services initially ran from Nuneaton (Trent Valley) to inconvenient termini at Overseal and Hugglescote. Eventually the Midland allowed its part-ner's trains to work through to Ashby, Burton and Coalville (Town from 1924). But agricultural hamlets such as Barton in the Beans and Belcher's Bar provided a very meagre pass-enger business which quickly fell victim to road competition. Nevertheless, when the LMS announced its intention to with-draw passenger services, the residents of Measham asked for a carriage to be attached to certain goods trains. Not surpris-ingly this request was refused and the last train for Shacker-stone left Ashby on the evening of Saturday 11 April 1931. In 1968 coal and goods traffic ceased too, and the route was aban-doned. However, local enthusiasts hope to restore Shacker-stone station to its Edwardian grandeur and create a small museum there, including a portrait of its most noble visitor, King Edward VII.

Charnwood Forest

As the line from Shackerstone curves towards Coalville Junction, the bulk of Bardon Hill appears on the eastern side. This 912ft summit marks the edge of a most attractive part of Leicestershire known as Charnwood Forest, where the red clay and coal seams are pierced by a series of ancient volcanic rocks. These tough slates and granites stand as wild bracken-covered crags overlooking lonely valleys where patches of the once extensive woodland remain. Charnwood certainly has beauty, but its rough slopes deterred settlement and stood as a barrier to canals and railways. Nevertheless, in 1874 the Charnwood Forest Company was incorporated to lay a single-track railway between Loughborough and the Ashby and Nuneaton line near Coalville. A direct route would have taken the metals across the forest, so from Whitwick the rails veered northwards, avoiding the 600ft summits but demanding sharp curves and numerous cuttings through the red sandstone which is banked against the ancient hills.

Whitwick heralded the scheme as the salvation of the whole district; optimism was gushing freely. But events even before the line was built set the tone for its whole career. During the ceremony marking the beginning of work on the railway at Loughborough in 1881, considerable amusement was caused when Mr E. M. P. de Lisle, squire of Garendon, had some difficulty in keeping his barrow on the plank provided when wheeling away the first sod. Soon after the line opened in 1883, the company found problems in keeping its own finances on the rails and was adjudged bankrupt in 1885. The shabby concern paid no dividends on ordinary shares throughout its existence, though the LNWR fared somewhat better. It had subscribed a third of the capital needed for construction of the line and worked it from the outset, taking half the receipts whatever the economic situation. By 1909 the gloom had lifted and the company left the hands of the receiver, remaining in charge of its own affairs until 1923 when it became part of the LMS.

In contrast to these hectic financial adventures, the track itself lay largely in the tranquil northern fringe of Charnwood Forest. Unfortunately, passengers were only a little more abundant than the shareholders' dividends and regular services were withdrawn in 1931. The delights of a trip on the 'Bluebell Line' had passed quietly away. Having left Loughborough Derby Road terminus (page 56) and climbed away from the town, Coalville trains approached the irregular Charnwood skyline. But beyond the opposite carriage window lay a sharply contrasting artificial landscape created by Garendon Hall. Although the mansion itself has now vanished, a Temple of Venus and Triumphal Arch incongruously decorate the hillside to recall its Palladian grandeur. Residents of Garendon, together with golfers bound for nearby Longcliffe, benefited from a halt opened at Snell's Nook in 1907 (499185). The service to this and contemporary halts at Grace Dieu and Thringstone was at first provided by an LNWR steam railcar which gave the impression of being an ordinary carriage but had a small vertical-boilered steam engine at one end. Trains were normally hauled by 2-4-2 side tank engines, though other LNWR locomotives such as 0-6-0s and 0-6-2 'Coal Tanks' coped with passenger as well as goods traffic on occasions.

At Shepshed, a village which sprawled into an industrial town during the nineteenth century, the railway provided a station which remains as one of the more interesting relics of the line (477186). A two-storey house adjoined the business part of the station which was a low building entered through a porch. Red brick and slate were employed, but a touch of ornament and three tall chimneys with bulbous tops gave some measure of individuality. Periodic excursions continued to bring life to the platforms until the early 1950s, but a scheme mooted at the turn of the century would, if carried out, have led to considerable activity. A link between Shepshed and the Great Central line north of Loughborough might have resulted in some interesting cross-country train workings.

Beyond Shepshed the trains ambled round the northern

Loughborough Derby Road and Ratby stations
(*the former from a photograph by Professor A. G. Ford*)

edge of Charnwood Forest, without a doubt the most delightful part of the journey. An impression of the view to which
passengers were treated can be gained from Tickhill Lane
overbridge (463186). A mile to the south lie the harsh crags
of High Sharpley and the rugged outline of Gun Hill with
the tip of a gaunt, derelict lodge peeping over the rocks.
Towards humped Ives Head squats the tower of Mount St
Bernard's Abbey, and in the foreground rests the restored
windmill at Blackbrook. On the opposite side of the railway
the Trent lowlands stretch away, and in the distance steam
billows from the huge power stations built in an age the
passengers never knew. Just here the trackbed was formed
over the ill-fated Charnwood Forest canal and a brick aqueduct over a farm lane has been used to carry the railway
(459185). Another halt overlooked the beautiful ruins of
Grace Dieu Nunnery and no doubt the tourist potential of
these sylvan delights became a consideration during the
leisured Edwardian years. But, whereas the ancient buildings
were of granite, the three-arch viaduct over the road was built
of red brick and developed an undignified sag before it was
demolished in 1967.

Beyond Thringstone trains entered a colliery district and
the landscape changed to an industrial one. Whitwick, a small
town built on undulating ground where the coal-bearing rocks
end abruptly against the Charnwood Hills, was approached
along a narrow gorge past City of Three Waters. Between here
and City of Dan the station was built. It was conveniently
situated near the town centre, but in a cramped cutting which
required the demolition of several cottages before it could be
excavated. Most of the buildings still remain as does a wooden
stairway which led from the tiny forecourt to the solitary
platform. Despite its present weed-choked slumber the station
has experienced considerable activity. Although the local
trains were sparsely used towards the end, business was somewhat more brisk on market days in Coalville and Loughborough or when Shepshed Wakes and Loughborough Fair
arrived. But some local youngsters were a bit too lively and

severed window straps found employment in many homes as razor strops for father, and excellent ones they made too!

Ambling past brickworks and collieries, the trains approached Coalville having taken 30 minutes for the 9½ miles from Loughborough. Unlike the Midland station which had a central site on the main thoroughfare, Coalville East hid away behind the trees at the end of a quiet street overlooked by Bardon Hill. Its buildings were similar to those at Shepshed until they were demolished in 1970.

Since its redundancy the Charnwood Forest railway has been covered by houses at Whitwick and a factory in Shepshed. A colliery tip spills over it near Coalville and the alignment through East station may be used for a bypass. Beyond Snell's Nook the motorway has completely wiped out the railway route and as traffic roars by it is hard to imagine the railcar chugging along. Whereas the trains crept round the Charnwood heights, adding a touch of local character and disturbing little, the new road tears relentlessly through the once secluded and quiet valleys.

A Loop Through Swadlincote

The final length of conventional passenger railway to be based on the Leicester to Burton route was almost contemporary with the Charnwood Forest line. Scenically and economically however they were far apart, for the Swadlincote loop passed almost entirely through a built up area and served numerous industrial concerns by an intricate network of branches. Along this stretch of the Leicestershire–Derbyshire border lies a belt of hilly ground where exploitation of local coal and a suitable clay permitted a brick, tile and pipe industry to flourish. This transformed tiny agricultural settlements into straggling towns while completely new communities sprang up around the collieries and brickworks. By 1880, Gresley, Newhall, Midway and Woodville had virtually coalesced to form a sprawling built up area centred on Swadlincote.

As the Burton line ran west of the high ground it avoided

this growing district, but in 1848 a spur was constructed along the broad Cadley Valley to serve Swadlincote. Subsequently a second branch opened from Swainspark, where the main line descends into Gresley tunnel, and climbed to Woodville, then rejoicing in the name of Wooden Box. Eventually it was decided that a through route would be advantageous and the two stubs became springing points for a new line. Most of the loop, together with stations at Swadlincote and Woodville, opened for passengers in 1883, though the track south of Woodville was not ready until 1884. Difficult country was encountered, so despite stiff gradients, tight curves and substantial cuttings, two tunnels (Woodville 307yd and Midway 104yd) were required where ridges barred the way.

Although the original branches were intended for industrial traffic, passengers were not ignored. Services to Swadlincote began in 1851, and trains used the old Woodville terminus for 25 years until they were diverted into the new station. At first the loop services retained branch line character with local trains travelling from Burton to Woodville or Ashby, though it later became usual for certain main line workings to interrupt their journey and visit Swadlincote. Such trains were hauled by a variety of motive power from 0–6–0 tender engines to smart LMS 2–6–4 passenger tanks (page 51). However, the tedious meandering between slag heaps and brick kilns did little to encourage customers. Local services declined steadily and when they ceased altogether only one train a week, a Saturday Leicester to Burton working, remained. Seaside excursions continued to run, but when the summer Saturday Desford to Blackpool train forsook the loop in 1962, its stations finally retired. Both have now been demolished, though use has been made of Swadlincote's westbound platform as a retaining wall between the fire station and a new housing estate. However, something more substantial remains at the original Woodville terminus where the vaguely Gothic station house is still occupied (315194).

Industrial traffic from a complex of private railways based on the original branches once provided considerable sustenance for the loop, but even this has virtually disappeared. Local works now rely on road transport and the curious North Staffordshire Railway Stoke to Wellingborough goods which plodded this way is long extinct. One short section west of Swadlincote thrives on coal from Cadley Colliery, but elsewhere the cinder trackbed, overgrown cuttings and defunct bridges lie forlorn. A fine impression of the railway in its context may be gained south of Woodville tunnel where the industrial landscape through which the line threaded is grim indeed (316184). Colliery tips and winding gear form a skyline, but the tall brickworks chimneys dominate everything including terraces of brick cottages, some deserted and miserably cracked by subsidence. Every gap seems to be filled with derelict ground where farmland has been abandoned or old clay pits lie choked with brambles. Within this unabashed ugliness the forgotten loop serves as a dump for industrial waste, shunned by all except a few adventurous children.

Trams and Tubs

Even when the loop was operational it failed to satisfy the transport requirements of Swadlincote and further developments were forthcoming. Evidence of these survives at Newhall where, by the side of a road optimistically named Sunnyside, stands a rusting iron post whose ornamental base bears a coat of arms and the legend 'Midland Railway Company' (286211). Responsibility for this enigma lies with a long abandoned electric tramway known as the Burton and Ashby Light Railways. Both Leicester and Burton-on-Trent had conventional street tramways, but the Burton and Ashby, though employing urban-type double-deck cars, was unique. Not only was it built and operated by the Midland Railway, but it deserted public roads at Newhall and pursued its own way across the fields for nearly a mile.

Agitation for such a system to serve industrial South Derbyshire began at the turn of the century, but naturally the Midland were concerned that it would erode their own traffic on the loop line. After squabbling between interested parties, it was the Midland themselves who applied for a Light Railway Order. This was granted in 1902, construction began three years later, and trams first entered Swadlincote on 13 June 1906.

There was nobody to cut a ribbon across the rails or break a bottle of best Burton brown ale over the bows of the first car on that summer day, but the South Derbyshire miners and their families, all set for an orgy of 'tramming', more than made up for it. Such were the scenes of wild excitement on the overloaded cars that the constabulary had to be summoned to restore order. Numerous jolly little episodes typified the line's heyday, such as the Saturday night when two trams came face to face on the single track at Sunnyside. The car from Burton was packed with merry colliers who had spent the evening swilling away pit dust with the local brew. Both drivers refused to reverse to their previous passing place and as tempers rose and faces turned scarlet the passengers hooted and cheered their respective sympathies. Eventually the eastbound car gave way and the other clattered triumphantly by, its occupants issuing a thunderous chorus of jubilation!

The open-top trams became a popular rendezvous during the 1920s and many a romance blossomed as the cool breeze of a summer evening blew across the fields. But the cold winds of an economic depression were also blowing, and in 1927 the trams were withdrawn. Although the system was rapidly dismantled, its passage through the fields and between the houses at Newhall has left numerous traces to delight those with the patience to search them out. Car sheds at Swadlincote are now National Coal Board workshops, while a nearby bridge built to carry trams over the loop line continues to bear road traffic. Although boundary posts, ornamental gates and several poles which once supported the overhead wires can be discovered in and around Newhall, the most obvious relic survives near Ashby station. In front of this grand building lie two lengths of track on which Midland tramcars once waited for Midland trains.

Though there is no longer a passenger service between Leicester and Burton, coal trains still trundle over the Coalville level crossing and delay rush hour traffic. Industry has been the lifeblood of railways west of Leicester ever since the first Leicester and Swannington train bore banners exclaiming:

Cheap coal and granite; warm hearths and good roads; may the triumphs of science prove the blessing of the people.

The colliery lines at Ibstock, Whitwick and Bagworth and the Groby granite railway, all of which opened in 1832, were the earliest of scores of branches serving quarries, pits, mines and factories between Leicester and Burton, where the many breweries had their own network.

One particularly interesting little line ran from the large Cliffe Hill granite quarries near Markfield to exchange sidings with the Midland, south of Bardon station. In 1894 the quarry firm received a substantial contract for track ballast and decided to replace its steam road tractors with a narrow-gauge railway which opened in 1897. By 1901 five Bagnall locomotives were at work on the $2\frac{1}{2}$ mile line and handled up to fourteen steel side-tipping 'tubs' laden with chippings. But gradients as severe as 1 in 29 required considerable care, as did the sharp curves where trains were often derailed. Eventually the toughest gradients were eased and in 1911 a deviation line on a high embankment overlooking Stanton was built to avoid the worst bends (469110). The strangest locomotive to enter service was a Sentinel geared steam engine which crashed on its first trial run in 1927. During the previous year's coal strike the locomotives must have made themselves particularly irksome as old solid rubber tyres from lorries were burnt as fuel. Yet, during 1927, it was decided to fit engines with bells as their steam whistles frightened the cattle!

Though this railway was abandoned in March 1948, many of its earthworks remain and rails are still in place across Billa

Barrow Lane where they have been polished, not by steel wheels, but by road vehicles (464114). Now the Cliffe Hill line has been erased from the map in common with so many of the once busy railway routes west of Leicester. Even the Midland Red bus services which replaced most of the old passenger trains are themselves rapidly losing customers as people acquire their own transport. Distant indeed are the days when Shepshed or Glenfield stations were an indispensable part of life in their respective villages.

CHAPTER 3

Between Syston and Peterborough

Lord Harborough's Curve

Although passenger trains no longer operate westwards from Leicester to Burton on Trent, it is still possible to enjoy the journey eastwards to Peterborough along a railway rich in historic interest and aesthetic quality. The Syston & Peterborough line was planned soon after the Midland company came into being and formed part of an urgent expansion programme designed to counter territorial advances by rival concerns, in this case the London & York which materialised as the Great Northern main line. Though the s & p was more or less a contemporary of the Burton line, any similarity between them ends there. Not only did the former encounter fierce opposition from an ageing aristocrat, but the landscape through which this railway passed was an agrarian one, unblemished by the spoils of mining. Instead of miserable colliery townships there are isolated farms, a scattering of idyllic villages and three old market towns whose history stretches back through the centuries. In order to accommodate Melton Mowbray, Oakham and Stamford the s & p adopted a circuitous route which also managed to avoid the highest ground.

The gentle Wreake Valley afforded the Midland an easy

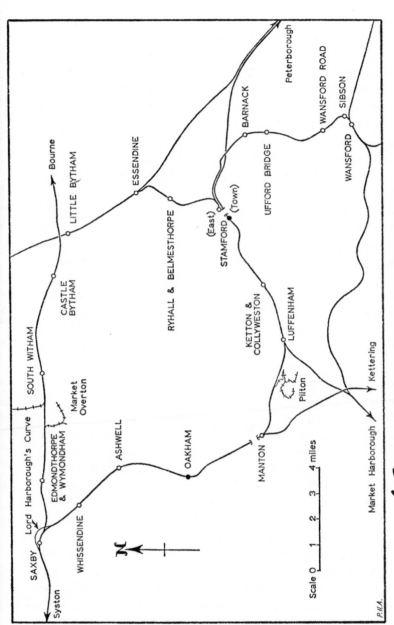

— Map of the railways between Syston and Peterborough

passage to Melton in marked contrast to the stiff climb over the windy uplands of High Leicestershire which faced Great Northern trains from Belgrave Road. Apart from Holwell ironworks and the occasional gravel pit there is no industry in the valley. The pastoral landscape with church spires peeping above dark fox coverts and ancient willows bowing over meandering brooks remains unspoilt. In such a setting lies Saxby, a farming hamlet four miles east of Melton. The passenger station which served this tiny community until 1961 was not one of the picturesque buildings erected when the railway was laid but a standard Midland structure dating from 1892 (813192). It opened with a new section of line designed to alleviate the sharp curve whose deserted cuttings and overgrown embankments can still be seen nearby. These derelict earthworks, insignificant as they appear today, are monuments to a bitter dispute between the local landowner and those promoting the railway. Parliamentary feuds were not uncommon: it will be recalled for instance that the Great Northern had to pacify the hunting fraternity during its attempts to reach Leicester. But the physical conflict which took place at Saxby was in a different class.

Lord Harborough, whose property lay in the path of the proposed line, disliked railways. This one was particularly irksome as it threatened to ruin his favourite views as well as bleed traffic from the Oakham Canal in which he was a major shareholder. Consequently, his response to a Midland approach concerning the purchase of land was to display notices along the borders of his estate emphasising that any attempt to survey Stapleford Park would be resisted with force. The ensuing 'Battle of Saxby' makes humorous reading now, but in 1844 it was a deadly serious affair.

Trouble began on Wednesday 13 November 1844 as seven Midland men approached the canal towpath. When ordered away by Lord Harborough's men the surveyors refused as they were still outside the Park. Nevertheless, nine armed estate workers 'arrested' the railwaymen, bundled them into a cart and wheeled them off to the local magistrate. When the unlawfulness of this act was pointed out by a policeman the head keeper tipped his prisoners out on to the roadway causing, among other things, some sore tempers! Despite their shaking, the Midland men returned the next day, their numbers swelled to forty by a batch of muscular navvies from Stamford and a few prize-fighters from Nottingham. This time Lord Harborough's men formed a solid barrier through which the railway contingency, with their backs to the opposition, attempted to break. Several men were forced up in the air so that they rolled over the heads of the other participants and eventually the whole absurd commotion ended up in a filthy ditch where the two sides became almost indistinguishable. The fracas ended with a chase along the towpath to the jubilation of the crowd of spectators who had enjoyed an excellent morning's entertainment.

Yet more fighting occurred on the following Saturday when a small party of Midland men emerged from the early morning shadows to conclude their survey. This time Lord Harborough's men included a hefty lock-keeper who demolished six challengers with single blows. In the general brawl which followed, the railway men suffered severe injuries and retreated with their smashed equipment. These three days of bedlam resulted in a spell in Leicester gaol for several navvies found guilty of riot and fines for Harborough's employees who had damaged surveying equipment.

Despite such opposition the Midland obtained its Act for the s & P line on 30 June 1845, but still Lord Harborough refused to allow construction work to begin. In an effort to please this most difficult of landowners the surveyors attempted to take measurements for a deviation which would carry the metals further away from Stapleford Hall. Once again they were challenged and on 28 November 1845 an army of 150 railwaymen were involved in a free-for-all during which his lordship drove a carriage at full speed into the opposition. Even when the new line became law during 1846 further difficulties lay ahead. The Act stipulated a tunnel under Cuckoo Plantation, one of Lord Harborough's favourite spinneys, but it proved to be too shallow and collapsed during construction taking most of the trees with it. Naturally, Harborough was furious and brought an action against the Midland resulting in yet another deviation Act which was passed on 22 July 1847. His lordship was finally beaten, but the troublesome middle section of the S & P did not open until 1848, almost two years after the rest of the line.

If one stands on the site of Saxby station and gazes across at the hills rolling away towards High Leicestershire it is easy to appreciate the concern Lord Harborough felt for the peace and beauty of Stapleford Park. The prospect of a new motorway wrecking an attractive piece of countryside raises even more opposition today. But in 1880 the severe curve became a nuisance to expresses using the freshly opened route between Nottingham and Kettering via Melton and Manton (see Chapter 6), so a more reasonable successor to the deceased peer allowed the Midland to build the easier curve now in use. There is plenty to see of the old line. Most of its grassy trackbed can be covered on foot and evidence of the Oakham Canal, once the scene of so much activity, can still be seen in the fields. The original half-timbered Saxby station survives as does an attractive gatekeeper's cottage where the rails crossed Stapleford Lane (page 187).

Tracks to Coast and Quarry

Almost as soon as it became disused, the original curve was severed by a new stretch of railway which branched from the S & P at Saxby and headed across the lonely limestone uplands into Lincolnshire. This line was once a favourite route to the sea for the inhabitants of the East Midlands and its metals carried countless thousands of holidaymakers bound for a fortnight at Great Yarmouth, Cromer or Hunstanton.

In 1893 several minor railways in Lincolnshire and Norfolk were combined to form the Midland and Great Northern Joint system which desperately required a link with Leicester and Nottingham. Such was the origin of the railway between

Saxby and Bourne. Though constructed by the Midland as far east as Little Bytham, where a massive girder bridge crossed the GNR main line (016177), the new route was an extension of the M & GN, by whom it was operated, rather than a local branch line of the larger company.

Wayside farming communities were provided with quite generous passenger facilities, especially at Wymondham where the main station building was a neat and compact structure identical to that at Saxby. Courses of blue brick and terracotta mouldings relieved the red brick walls whereas the waiting room was timbered up to waist level on its platform side and the remainder glazed. In front of this was a small canopy formed by a continuation of the roof supported on two wooden posts. Three tall, slender chimneys completed the design. Though derelict for some time after its closure, this attractive station has been saved from demolition and converted into a most desirable bungalow (page 52).

Passenger services began in 1894 with three local trains each way daily. This seemingly meagre provision was quite sufficient for such a rural railway as some of the stations on the older lines east of Bourne served little more than scattered farmsteads on the blustery Fens. Long distance traffic proved to be far more remunerative and the through expresses from Leicester to Great Yarmouth which also began in 1894 were such a conspicuous success that twenty years later they were conveying portions from Derby and Nottingham with through carriages to Norwich and Lowestoft. These trains introduced the M & GN 'Yellowbellies' (a nickname derived from their distinctive livery) to the East Midlands. There were plenty of seasonal trains too, and with the growing popularity of holiday camps during the 1950s excursions ran from Mansfield, Shirebrook and Erewash Valley stations as well as the big cities.

Seaside trains certainly prospered but stopping services received little revenue and though station yards were often well stacked with agricultural produce this traffic was hardly sufficient to support the line. The entire M & GN system had become grossly uneconomic and in 1959 passenger facilities were withdrawn from 160 miles of it, including the extension to Saxby. Through trains such as the fast freights conveying vegetables and fruit from rich Fenland farms to the city markets used alternative routes and eventually the rails between Saxby and Bourne were lifted except for a short section giving access to Market Overton ironstone quarries. The spectacle of heavily-laden holiday trains tackling the gradient out of Saxby became just a memory.

The Market Overton branch was one of many single track railways threading unexpectedly through the Rutland and Lincolnshire farmland to serve remote quarries, for these limestone hills contain rich iron deposits and have been etched with numerous winding gorges where this raw material has been excavated. Heavy trains of the orange-brown stone bound for blast furnaces at Stanton and Staveley still roll along the Syston & Peterborough line today.

As with other quarry lines, the Market Overton system was originally operated by steam locomotives and perhaps winter saw them at their most impressive. In the grey dusk of a bitter January day a powerful dark green saddle tank waited at the head of fifteen steel wagons piled high with stone. A towering excavator stood engulfed in sulphurous smoke which rolled from the engine and away into the dim sky. Suddenly a yellow glare flooded the cab, highlighting the driver as he opened the firehole door to feed in more fuel for the final haul of the day. Harsh grating of shovel on coal was soon drowned by a piercing blast of steam from the safety valves indicating that the fierce ascent could begin. Sharp exhaust blasts shook the raw quarry walls until icy rails caused the driving wheels to slip and a muffled roar filled the darkening chasm. When after some minutes the effort was relaxed, the clattering of rail joints gave way to clanking buffers and grinding brakes. As the train came to a stand clear of the sheltered pit a cutting wind whipped over the dark fields to snatch smoke and steam from the simmering engine. When shunting had been completed and the locomotive stabled for the night the quarrymen could desert this bleak place for a well-deserved fireside chair.

Such a scene was commonplace some years ago but most quarries have now been abandoned and the few that do survive are worked by diesels. A particularly interesting system was that opened by the Staveley Company at Pilton in 1919 (922028). It was shunted by sturdy 0–6–0 saddle tanks and involved a steep descent to the exchange sidings on the s & p line. Controlling traffic from the Midland route was a centrally-pivoted board signal which permitted movement when swivelled parallel to the rails but halted it when facing oncoming trains. As with many similar sites, trains no longer ease cautiously through the damp, tree-lined cuttings and vegetation has run amok. Fortunately these small quarries have not had the same ruinous effect on the landscape that coal mining would have done and Rutland remains one of the least spoilt of English counties.

The Marquis of Exeter's Railway

Beyond Pilton the s & p line follows the River Chater to Ketton where an easy course along the Welland Valley is assumed. Before long the spires and towers of Stamford's ancient churches appear over the water meadows. To serve this attractive Lincolnshire market town the Midland built a delightful little station which remains open and still boasts a strange tower whose cupola bears a weather vane incorporating the legend 's & pr'.

Stamford once enjoyed the services of another station tucked away in a quiet part of the town alongside the River Welland. Masked by trees and flanked by old cottages lay East station, once the terminus of two short Great Northern branches (034069). This lavishly designed building tried hard to conceal its true function for it had all the trappings of a modest Elizabethan mansion including mullioned windows, clusters of pompous chimneys, a host of stone finials and a squat tower which served to relieve the otherwise symmetrical appearance.

Protecting the small forecourt was a row of railings incorporating a gate whose posts displayed some intricate ironwork, a
feature in which the GNR seemed to take great pride.

The main hall was an ornate affair with lashings of carved
woodwork and a gallery rich in decorative iron. Beyond it the
prospective passenger entered a neat shed covering two tracks,
one either side of a central platform, and at one time it was
possible to see both lines occupied by trains awaiting their
respective departure times. That on the left was prepared for
a ten-minute journey to Essendine while the other would take
a leisurely 25 minutes to reach Wansford. Such were the
modest local services provided by the Stamford & Essendine
Railway which built this elaborate terminus (page 52).

It remains controversial whether the GNR main line from
King's Cross to the North avoided Stamford for purely topo-
graphical reasons or because the Marquis of Exeter, whose
large estate lay near the town, adopted a similar attitude to
Lord Harborough. Whichever the case this important coach-
ing stage on the Great North Road suffered as a result. In an
effort to reverse Stamford's decline and perhaps expiate his
earlier sins the Marquis supported a locally promoted link
with Essendine on the GNR. As an indication of his participa-
tion, the Exeter coat-of-arms was incorporated in the stone
gables of Stamford station which already had a strong affinity
with Burghley House where the Marquis resided.

Soon after the railway opened in 1856 it became clear that
most passengers wished to travel southwards and a link with
Peterborough was proposed. Unfortunately this enterprise
materialised as a rural branch to Wansford, an obscure place
on the LNWR line from Northampton. But the S & E seemed
to revel in unfortunate episodes for besides facing away from
Peterborough the new line stopped short of Wansford for a
time while disputes with Euston were ironed out. This
necessitated a separate station which was little more than an
absurdly remote platform in the fields bearing the name
Sibson (096982).

Once clear of Stamford station the parallel Essendine and

Wansford tracks ran alongside s & p metals which had tunnelled under the old part of the town. A crossover was controlled by both Midland and GNR signal boxes, the latter perched precariously above the River Welland. It was here that a GNR 0–4–2 tank engine plunged ungraciously into the river and was nicknamed the 'Welland Diver'. The Essendine track then veered northwards, took an easy course up the Gwash Valley to Belmesthorpe and entered a long cutting through a ridge which barred the way to the main line. The only structure of any significance was a timber trestle spanning the Welland near St Leonard's Priory (041074). The fragility of this bridge had to be seen to be believed for in spite of its length supports were few and the weight of trains was taken by timber baulks held together by longitudinal girders. Ironically, the metal parapets had a classical column decoration which seemed apologetic for the inadequacy of the design. Although it carried two tracks the one nearest Stamford was a separate siding serving Priory goods depot and a number of industrial concerns.

Apart from a few bridges the Wansford line required very little engineering work for its path through the cornfields of Huntingdonshire. From Stamford it accompanied the s & p line on a low embankment for two miles whence it swept over the Midland by a girder bridge and cut across the fields to Barnack station (083053). This neat little structure was built of limestone using small pieces of dressed stone for the fabric and larger blocks for quoins. The chimneys were tall and splendid but even smaller features such as the pointed windows and doorways were beautifully executed. An identical building was erected in remote surroundings at Wansford Road (089996).

In the early 1920s a diminutive green 0–4–2 tank engine with a smart train of six-wheel teak carriages rattling through quiet farmland and pausing at trim wayside stations was accepted as part of an unchanging scene. But economically the operation was hopeless and even the bulkiest farmer had no trouble finding adequate space in the carriages. So passenger traffic over the Wansford branch ceased in 1929 by which time many trains ran completely empty. A few people missed the white smoke trailing across ploughed fields or through dark coppices but this quiet agricultural countryside never really needed a railway. Though the rails were lifted long ago almost every bridge is intact and both Barnack and Wansford Road stations survive: the former as offices, the latter as a dwelling. The route can still be traced throughout, albeit in some places a wilderness of brambles.

Several years elapsed before a similar fate overtook the Essendine branch. When the service was withdrawn in 1959 its trains were less colourful though still operated by antique equipment, usually an old GNR 4-4-2 tank engine with a few drab non-corridor coaches. Since 1957 trains had worked into Stamford Town, thus rendering East station redundant as a passenger terminus. Nevertheless it still exists and handsomely repays a visit. The main building has been converted into living accommodation whereas the train shed has acquired a new roof and serves as a warehouse.

At certain times of the day any attempt to admire Stamford's fine buildings is made virtually impossible by the stench and rattle of heavy traffic weaving through the narrow streets. In these circumstances it is worthwhile taking a stroll down Water Street to the stately old GNR terminus and contemplating the days when movement from one place to another was less hectic, even if somewhat inconvenient. At Essendine, where branch trains crept into a side platform, the most up-to-date expresses now roar past, their passengers oblivious to the remains of the Stamford & Essendine Railway.

Though the S & E has been discarded, the Syston and Peterborough route, which formed the theme of this chapter, continues to carry passengers. Its trains are not fast but the line has aesthetic qualities which make a journey along it well worthwhile. But gas lamps against elaborate ironwork, boxes of pigeons on platform barrows and historic stations in little market towns are not consistent with a prosperous modern railway, so a government grant is necessary to keep the service running. It seems very likely that before long Stamford will have two beautiful but forgotten stations.

CHAPTER 4

Central Leicestershire

A One-time Main Line

For nearly seventy years the public had a choice of railways between Rugby and Nottingham. One route had been opened back in 1840 by the Midland Counties company but the other was completed as late as 1899 by the Great Central Railway and proved to be the last new main line built in Britain. Paradoxically, most of the older route has been extensively modernised and now forms part of the Inter-City network whereas the newer one, which was always the faster and more popular of the two, lies derelict and forgotten.

The Midland Counties line opened from Trent Junction to Leicester on 5 May 1840, followed shortly by the extension southwards to Rugby where a junction was made with the pioneer London & Birmingham Railway. At first a considerable quantity of traffic passed this way, including the earliest expresses from northern England to London. But this importance was short lived for in 1857 the Midland Railway, which had inherited the Midland Counties, opened the Hitchin line as the first part of an independent route to the capital, and during 1864 the South Leicestershire Railway established a more direct link between Leicester and Birmingham. Consequently the section between Wigston and Rugby was rapidly

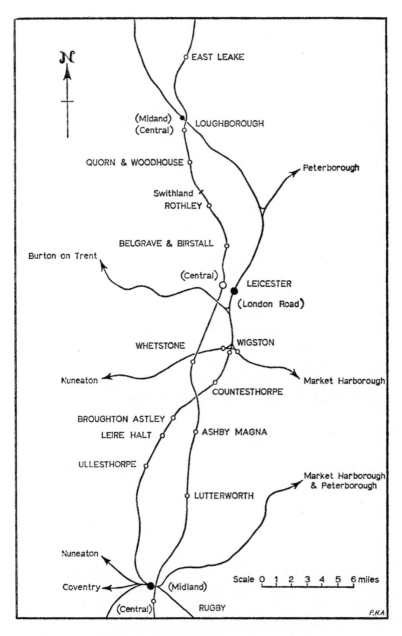

Map of the railways of Central Leicestershire

demoted to a local branch line, in which form it survived for nearly a century.

Wigston itself became an important junction and for many years possessed three passenger stations including that on the Rugby line which served South Wigston, a dismal township associated with the local hosiery industry. The platforms here, instead of facing each other, were staggered either side of a level crossing over the main street (page 85). Beyond Wigston the ground sloped away towards the Sence Valley which the railway crossed on a high embankment. Crow Mills viaduct spanned the river itself and though in later years this was a solid structure consisting of deep girders laid on blue brick piers the original was of much flimsier construction. In fact it was so feeble that the floods of 1852 washed it away and disaster was only avoided by the prompt action of a local miller who saw the bridge collapse and sounded the alert.

For the rest of its length the line passed through undulating agricultural countryside liberally sprinkled with sizeable farming villages, though at first only Countesthorpe, Broughton Astley and Ullesthorpe were considered worthy of a station. Railway houses survive at Broughton Astley and Ullesthorpe, that at the former place reflecting the style of the original Midland Counties' Campbell Street station in Leicester. The rails finally deserted the Soar Valley and began their descent through Warwickshire near a level crossing over Watling Street (499853). Drivers using this busy road were often frustrated by the long delay as an almost empty train sauntered past behind an old Midland 4-4-0 or an LMS 2-6-4 tank engine. At its southern extremity the branch strode across the River Avon by a graceful brick viaduct and finally joined the main line just west of Rugby station.

Some years after the line closed in 1962 there were suggestions that it might re-open as part of the extension of electrified lines into the East Midlands. But the formation was already severed by the motorway and obliterated by a factory at Wigston, houses at Countesthorpe and a garbage dump in the cutting just north of Rugby. Had the old trackbed not been disposed of so quickly the entire Midland Counties route might once again have become the main line to London.

The Last Main Line

In Roman times Leicester was a fortified settlement known as Ratae Coritanorum and fascinating remains dating from this period can still be examined at the Jewry Wall site in the city. But nearby there is one relic, a fine mosaic pavement, which is less conspicuously preserved, for during the 1890s it lay directly in the path of a new railway and only after persistent agitation by archaeologists was a special vault constructed so that the treasure could be preserved in situ. This unusual arrangement vividly illustrates how the Great Central Railway was thrust right through the ancient heart of the city and, in fact, added a fresh element to the urban landscape.

The Manchester, Sheffield & Lincolnshire Railway had been a lively provincial concern linking the Lancashire and Yorkshire coalfields with the east coast, but it was obliged to hand over a great deal of its traffic to rival companies which operated direct routes to London. The management was unhappy about this state of affairs and in 1873 expressed willingness to combine with the Midland in promoting a new railway to the capital. These plans foundered, as did several others during the following twenty years, but the MS & L never lost sight of its objective and in 1893 Parliament finally sanctioned an independent main line from the Nottinghamshire town of Annesley, where a branch from Beighton already existed, to Quainton Road in Buckinghamshire. By exercising running powers over the Metropolitan Railway to Finchley Road the MS & L could proceed to its own London terminus in Marylebone.

In keeping with its enhanced status the company changed its title to Great Central Railway and faced the twentieth century with dignity and optimism. But cynics claimed that if MS & L stood for money sunk and lost, GC meant gone completely, for the London extension did more than burn a hole in the pocket, it very nearly destroyed the whole wardrobe. Land costs in Leicester and Nottingham were colossal, numerous heavy engineering works were required, and the expenditure on rolling stock was so great that new locomotives had to be purchased through a finance company. Nevertheless the country gained a magnificent railway and the stretch through central Leicestershire was one of the few really fast main lines in the East Midlands.

Whereas the Midland Counties' tracks from Nottingham to Rugby adopted a meandering course taking advantage of natural routeways, the Great Central line linking these two towns was more or less straight, though the hilly ground encountered as a result demanded substantial earthworks as well as two short tunnels. North of Loughborough and south of Leicester the tracks swept boldly across undulating country with all the confidence brought by half a century of railway building experience, for contractors' locomotives and steam cranes shifted the clay in a manner undreamed of by the pioneers. The broad curves and gentle gradients (no steeper than 1 in 176) were designed as a racing ground for expresses, a function which they performed admirably.

Between Leicester and Loughborough the GCR passed close to Charnwood Forest and encountered a landscape of particular beauty. Beyond Birstall the medieval deer park at Bradgate came into view and occasional glimpses were to be had of the strange tower and arch known as Old John. Soon the railway strode across Swithland Reservoir by a low viaduct and used Brazil Wood, an insular rocky knoll, as a stepping stone (558137). On the left lay a grand prospect of the tree-covered south-eastern part of Charnwood with The Brand and Swithland Woods in the foreground and the craggy summit of Beacon Hill rising behind them. On the right lay the low whaleback of Buddon Wood, its granite slopes thick with bronze-coloured bracken and silver birch. A steam train added something special to this splendid panorama, especially very early on a cold morning when mist hung above the placid water and the trail of smoke from a speeding express drifted idly away through the winter trees.

Buildings and Bridges

Most passenger stations along the new line were constructed to an island design whereby both tracks diverged around a single platform on which waiting rooms and offices were built. Apart from those serving London and Nottingham, the most generous facilities were at Leicester Central, though both Rugby and Loughborough acquired sizeable stations. Even the smaller places were provided with neat little structures, that at Belgrave & Birstall serving as a fine example (588084).

A steady climb, mostly on high embankments, faced trains heading north from Leicester and by the time they reached Birstall, passengers could enjoy a fine view of the city spread out over the Soar Valley. The station marked the beginning of a huge cutting and when newly opened it lay out in the wilds almost a mile from each of the settlements it purported to serve. But as suburban Leicester engulfed the old villages Belgrave & Birstall station gained a great deal of new residential traffic.

The entrance was merely an archway built into the parapet of a bridge leading to the local golf course, but it incorporated a chimney from the porters' room and had a peculiar appearance. A covered stairway led down to the platform where prospective passengers were faced with the ticket window behind a barrier. Blue bricks were used for the bridge itself, but each little block of platform buildings was solidly made of orange bricks with sandstone slabs for the lintels (page 85). Marylebone expresses absolutely rocked the station as they burst from beneath the bridge and tore down the gradient into Leicester. Stopping trains were in less of a hurry as they were responsible for bringing scores of city workers home to outlying districts after a day's work and, as carriage doors slammed, the platforms of this obscure suburban station bustled with life.

Evidence of a station which might have been heavily used

had it ever opened for passengers remains at the Swithland to Rothley Road underbridge (563132). Though the GCR had visions of Swithland Reservoir as a recreation centre its plans were thwarted and work stopped on the unfinished passenger facilities. Nevertheless, the rails continued to veer round an imaginary platform and the bricked-up entrance can be seen under the bridge to this day. A compensatory shuttle service from Leicester to Woodhouse and Rothley was operated for the benefit of day-trippers at weekends and public holidays until the 1930s.

At Leicester the most spectacular part of the new line was a splendid viaduct which ran for more than a mile across the city. This complex and costly piece of engineering included 97 blue brick arches, 11 plate girders spanning various thoroughfares, 3 large lattice deck girders where the railway encountered the River Soar or its associated canal, and 2 magnificent bowstring lattice girders across Northgate Street and Braunstone Gate respectively. An incidental effect of this lofty passage was that travellers were treated to wonderful views of the old heart of the city, notably the Roman ruins, the Mercian Cathedral of St Nicholas and the slender spire of St Mary de Castro.

The line introduced trains into the everyday scene of Leicester as no railway had done previously and this was nowhere more apparent than at Braunstone Gate bridge. On sweltering July afternoons holiday trains from the south coast clattered towards the station and tanned young faces excitedly peered at familiar landmarks through the coach windows. With rush-hour traffic filling the glistening streets on a wet winter evening, London businessmen settled in comfortable seats as their express headed home and shrouded the girderwork with smoke and steam. As fog clamped down at the end of a chilly November day, local trains filled with weary shopworkers bound for Whetstone and Lutterworth rumbled across the steel plates and the carriage lamps cast dim beams of light into the grey murk. The moods were countless.

When the greater part of Leicester Central station was

Leicester Central station, exterior

being demolished in 1971 an Irish labourer exclaimed in no uncertain language that whoever built the place must have built the Pyramids, for practically every crowbar and hammer he had used on the tough ironwork had ended up somewhat worse for wear! The GCR no doubt expected their new station to survive for considerably longer than seventy years and designed the buildings accordingly, but the vacant space where it once stood is a sad tribute to the folly of those hopes.

The frontage was a respectable example of the Jacobean revival, then in full flush. It incorporated three large entrances flanked by groups of windows, a parapet formed of nine ornate gables, and a bulky clock tower capped by an onion-shaped cupola. The building was finished in orange bricks relieved by terracotta dressings and made quite a pleasant architectural contribution to the city (page 83). Behind this facade extended a glass-roofed concourse leading through to the booking hall, a lofty and cheerful place in marked contrast to the dismal subway by which passengers gained access to the trains. A flight of steps ascended to the ticket barrier which stood half way along a large island platform with two bays at each end. In addition there were passing loops for goods trains and, considering its constricted site on the viaduct, the station layout was very efficient. An extensive canopy dominated the squat buildings at this level, but these were carefully designed in the same style as those adjoining the street and incorporated both refreshment and dining rooms. Internally these rooms were luxuriously finished in brown and green vitrified tiles bearing a railway wheel motif, together with an abundance of dark woodwork. The restaurant was particularly splendid and when it closed on 29 December 1951 it still had the original fittings as well as plates, cutlery and crockery bearing the arms of the Great Central Railway.

Trains and Traffic

Because it was an extremely busy main line with important industrial and cross-country traffic, the London extension saw

Suburban Leicester: Plate 9 (above) 42615 guides a Leicester to Rugby Midland stopping train into one of the dingy staggered platforms at Wigston South on 21 July 1952; Plate 10 (below) a mixed freight heading south through Belgrave & Birstall

From splendour to humiliation: Plate 11 (above) *a brand-new Robinson 4–6–0, No 1167* Lloyd George, *speeds through Belgrave & Birstall with a Bradford to Marylebone express in 1921;* Plate 12 (below) *Leicester viaduct on 2 September 1966 with a London to Nottingham train in the evening shadows*

a greater variety of motive power and trains than any other railway in the East Midlands. As the years passed, obsolete engines were replaced by newer designs; ancient MS & L Sacré 4–4–0s found employment at first, but sixty years later the Bournemouth–York train was being hauled by the most modern Brush Type 4 diesels. Furthermore, at any one time Leicester depot had to house a range of engines to deal with every sort of traffic from pick-up goods to fast passenger.

Great Central expresses were undoubtedly at their finest during Edwardian times. The locomotives themselves were painted bright green with chocolate-brown splashers, vermillion buffer beams and yellow lining out, whereas the plush bogie carriages built for the new line carried a chocolate and pale grey livery lined out in gold, though this was replaced by a more serviceable varnished teak finish after a few years. A handsome Robinson 4–6–0 storming through the Leicestershire countryside with its immaculate coaches certainly presented a glorious sight (page 86).

Local passenger trains were hauled by almost every type of locomotive from goods tanks commandeered in an emergency to newly outshopped express engines being run-in. A couple of somewhat unsuccessful steam rail cars were once employed between Leicester, Rugby and Loughborough, whereas, by way of a contrast, the world-famous and much-admired Pacific *Flying Scotsman* has, on at least one occasion, worked a Leicester to Rugby stopping train while in a most unglamorous condition awaiting an overhaul.

Through trains from the south coast via Banbury and Woodford regularly brought Great Western locomotives to Leicester, and bank holiday or sporting specials were occasionally hauled by Southern engines. During World War II troop trains often had streamlined LNER Pacifics in charge, including *Mallard*, the world's fastest steam locomotive. The most unconventional machine seen at Leicester Central was GT3, a gas-turbine engine which underwent a six-month trial during 1961. It was attractively painted in pale brown, but the exhaust fumes were so hot that they played havoc with overhead equipment and once set fire to the smoke shields on Northgate Street bridge.

So, the Great Central was a heavily used yet outstandingly efficient line with more than its share of variety. But despite the hard work, perhaps because of it, Leicester Central men had a down-to-earth joviality exemplified by the nicknames they gave each other: Razza, Sitha, Shuteye, Chinum, Sticky and Mashum, to name but a few. Likewise, drivers and firemen rarely referred to engines, especially the older ones, by their formal classifications but gave them such evocative titles as Bulldogs and Jumbos; Glenalmonds and Pom-Poms; Big Tinies and Jersey Lillies; Ragtimers and Chinese Crackers. One particular shunter, who constantly seemed to be on the receiving end of good-natured leg-pulls about such items as gas radios, happened to amble along towards a group of his mates who were examining an owl which had flown into the path of a Marylebone express and had spent the rest of the journey to Leicester on the front running plate. After a little persuasion he went away beaming, convinced that the bird was a flat-faced pheasant and would make a very juicy supper!

As might be expected with such a large volume of traffic using the relatively restricted track space at Leicester, there were one or two mishaps. In 1931 two engines involved in shunting movements collided at the north end of the station and one of them almost fell into the small Quakers' cemetery alongside the line. The following year a train being propelled into one of the bays mounted the platform and threatened to demolish the gentlemen's lavatory. But one of the worst accidents occurred on 25 September 1949 near Northgate Street bridge, and even today the patched-up viaduct parapet bears witness to those distant events (582051).

Percy Banyard had driven the 6.55pm stopping passenger train from Woodford to Leicester where the locomotive, B1 class 4-6-0 61108, was detached from the train and moved forward beyond a cross-over on the viaduct. When given the signal it would switch tracks and run back through the station towards the engine shed, a manoeuvre which had been accomplished daily without a hitch but which on this occasion resulted in disaster. Percy awaited the signal, but a semi-fast passenger train from Nottingham was given the all-clear and after a few minutes it rattled safely past into the station. This was an opportune moment for the B1 to move, but the signalman had forgotten about his light engine which, in the dusk, was barely visible behind the massive bridge girders. Instead he cleared the signals for a fully laden southbound coal train which took some time to arrive and trundle through the station.

At this point the signalman made a frightening move. He pulled the levers giving right-of-way to an empty coal train from Woodford to Annesley which had followed the stopping passenger train under clear signals. By now Percy was sounding the continuous pop-pop emergency whistle, though a distant rumble emphasised that any move would have to be a rapid one. The gruff exhaust beats gradually grew louder and out of the gloom appeared the rugged outline of a Robinson GCR 2–8–0, its billowing smoke illuminated by the station lights. Suddenly the signalman realised his error, dashed across the cabin and wrenched the levers, but already the powerful engine was thundering past his window on to the bridge.

As the points clicked Percy desperately slammed his engine into reverse gear and opened the regulator, but time had run out and there followed an impact which shook a large part of Leicester. The crew of 63862, which tore into the other engine and turned it on its side, had seen the danger ahead and jumped clear. This was just as well, for after the collision their charge veered to the left, smashed through the parapet and landed at the back of Tommy Wadsworth's fishing tackle shop, bringing some of the building down with it. Percy Banyard was rescued from his cab with remarkably few injuries, though his engine hung precariously over the edge of the viaduct and lay buried beneath upturned wagons. As the debris was being cleared, all sorts of strange things came to light including several squashed cars, and in his shop window

Wadsworth displayed a photograph of the uninvited guest in his back yard and added the appropriate caption, 'We caught this one!'

Epitaph

It had been feared for some time before the railways were nationalised that the Great Central main line was not to have the prolonged healthy future predicted by its promoters. But in 1948 its eradication became merely a matter of time, for the London extension had been born out of rivalry between independent companies when traffic was abundant. Once a unified network was created this element of competition no longer existed and a duplicate route mostly through unremunerative agricultural countryside became surplus to requirements. Decline set in during the 1950s but accelerated after the once-cherished express service between Marylebone and Manchester was withdrawn in 1961. Most local stations closed two years later but the Nottingham to London semi-fast trains, which at one stage consisted of totally unsuitable non-corridor diesel railcars, survived until 1966 (page 86).

Leicester Central, which had already lost its refreshment facilities and had been ruined externally by a hideous brick parapet erected in place of the Jacobean gables, then became an unstaffed halt. Diesel railcars ambled between Rugby and Nottingham for almost another three years, but they lurched along deteriorating track and stopped at dilapidated stations with boarded–up windows and decaying platforms where nature was fighting back. On 3 May 1969 a large crowd filled the bleak platforms at Leicester Central to see the last train depart and lamented the end of an era. But though a decorative lintel over the parcels office entrance still bore the inscription 'Great Central Railway' and a preservation society expressed a wish to re-open part of the redundant line, the days when the 4.30am newspaper train covered the $22\frac{1}{2}$ miles to Arkwright Street, Nottingham, in 22 minutes had vanished long before.

CHAPTER 5

High Derbyshire

The High Peak Trail

Some of the loveliest and most remote parts of the East Midlands are to be found in the hilly district which extends northwards from Derby towards Manchester and Sheffield and forms the southern extremity of the great Pennine range. Much of this area has been incorporated in the Peak District National Park and it contains two very different types of scenery: the high gritstone moors of the north and the rolling limestone uplands which constitute the bulk of the region covered by this chapter.

Despite physical difficulties and the scarcity of population, there were strong incentives for railway construction in High Derbyshire. Firstly, the profitable exploitation of limestone, lead and fluorspar reserves was only possible with an efficient transport system; secondly, direct communication between the densely settled parts of Lancashire and the East Midlands involved crossing the country in which Buxton, Bakewell, Ashbourne and Matlock were the only towns. The railway system which did eventually develop, though considerably less intense than in other parts of the East Midlands, was one of especial interest, not only historically but also from the point of view of its engineering.

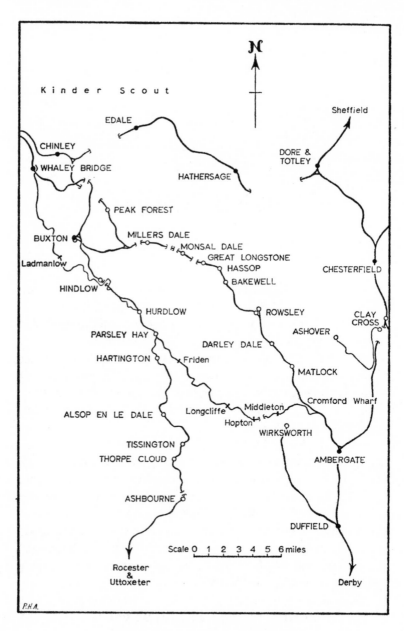

Map of the railways of High Derbyshire

In 1799 a horse tramway was opened from the Peak Forest Canal at Buxworth to extensive limestone quarries in Doveholes Dale, but the first line to make a complete transect of the Peak District was the celebrated Cromford & High Peak Railway which deservedly enjoyed the attentions of numerous writers and enthusiasts. The original plan was to extend the Peak Forest Canal south-eastwards to join the Cromford Canal, thus forming a navigable channel between the industrial areas of Cheshire and Derbyshire, but the prospect of expensive structural works and the strong likelihood of inadequate water supplies on the porous limestone hills put paid to the idea.

Instead, it was decided to link the two canals by means of a 33-mile long railway which took six years to construct and became fully operational in 1831. These were pioneer days and as there were no comparable lines from which to take a lead the engineer, Josias Jessop, followed canal practice by creating long, almost level sections connected by inclined planes, the equivalent of lock-flights, where wagons were raised or lowered by a wire rope, usually driven by a stationary steam engine. Between the inclines the C & HPR clung to the contours and so largely avoided heavy earthworks, though at the expense of some exceedingly tight curves, notably that at Gotham (page 103).

The level stretches were at first worked by horses and an interesting relic of this era is the station house at Longcliffe where the original stables can still be seen (225557). Steam locomotives began to take over after only a few years however, and this form of motive power reigned supreme until the system closed. Because of the very nature of the line, engines allocated to the C & HPR had to be relatively small and LNWR 'Chopper' 2–4–0 tanks, ex-North London Railway 0–6–0 tanks and ex-War Department 0–6–0 saddle tanks have all, at one time or another, been characteristic of these tracks across the Derbyshire hills.

The C & HPR was absorbed by the LNWR in 1887 and the section of line between Ladmanlow and Shallcross abandoned shortly afterwards. Nevertheless, the remainder survived until after nationalisation and still used some of the original machinery for working the inclines. Even after the last train ran in 1967 the railway remained rich in industrial archaeology. Some of the most interesting features were undoubtedly the inclines themselves: that at Sheep Pasture near the southern end of the line for example (311560). Runaways seem to have been characteristic of this particular gradient and in 1888 two vehicles shot off the tracks, across the Cromford Canal and over the Midland main line, just beyond which they were smashed to pieces in a field. To prevent a repetition of this hair-raising event a 'catch-pit' was dug near the bottom of the slope and the running rails made to veer round it. Any train over which control was lost could be directed into here, and the ruins of one wagon testify to the usefulness of this device.

Two miles further west lay Middleton incline, from the exposed summit of which there were magnificent views over towards Wirksworth and the Derwent Valley (275552). One feature of outstanding interest which still survives here is the original winding engine, a twin-cylinder beam type dating from 1825. Together with the stone building which houses it and forms a prominent landmark, this ancient machine has been preserved and beautifully restored. Hopton incline was also worked by means of a stationary engine at first, but during 1877 the approach was modified to allow locomotives to ascend unassisted (253546). Nevertheless, part of the climb still stood at 1 in 14 and for many years this was the most severe railway gradient in Britain climbed by adhesion alone. It was most exhilarating to watch two steam engines attacking it together with a loaded train, for their exhausts rose in tremendous plumes and the sound echoed around the hills.

Of the remaining inclines, one of unusual interest was that at Whaley Bridge (012814). Until 1952 it gave rail access to a couple of mills by the canal and right until the end a horse gin rather than a stationary engine was employed for lifting the wagons. The animal was harnessed to a beam which was affixed to a vertical spindle and this in turn drove a horizontal pulley through a pinion and gear wheel.

There were three tunnels on the c & HPR and even these provided plenty of variety. Hopton tunnel (266548) was bored through an abrupt limestone ridge which barred the way and suffered from excessive dampness through lack of a brick lining. Its flat-arched section was a tight squeeze for locomotives and the massive approach cuttings were gaunt, craggy excavations. Newhaven tunnel (151629) merely served to carry the line under the Ashbourne to Buxton road, but it is of particular interest by virtue of the strange carvings above each of its portals. One of these depicts a primitive wagon and the other the company coat-of-arms. Burbage tunnel (032738) stood on the long-abandoned northern section. It was drilled through tough gritstone and its badly decayed northern portal may still be examined by tramping either along the sodden trackbed from Goyt's Bridge or over the desolate peat bog appropriately known as Wild Moor.

For several years there was a passenger service over the c & HPR, but this came to an end in 1877 after a fatal accident. The public travelled in a 'fly' coach attached to goods trains but the journey took anything up to six hours and must have been incredibly tedious for the ordinary traveller. A service which proved to be of greater value was the transport of water in rail tankers converted from old locomotive tenders. This reflected the water shortage on the limestone uplands, and though a great deal of this commodity was used for engine purposes some was supplied to factories and quarries and some was provided for domestic use, the cottagers fetching their quota from tankers shunted into sidings along the route.

The remaining traffic was largely associated with the industrial establishments which grew up alongside the line. Unfortunately these had a disfiguring effect on the otherwise pleasant countryside; notable offenders were Friden brickworks, Hopton boneworks and certain of the limestone quarries. However, by using the railway these concerns ensured its survival for much longer than would have been the case had only through freight been carried.

The C & HPR was a wonderful anachronism. Even now there is ample to interest the explorer and it will soon be possible to walk along much of the trackbed with ease, for this is being converted into a footpath to be known as the High Peak Trail. But there are certain things that have gone for good. It is most unlikely that the smell of steam and hot oil will return to the Middleton engine for instance, and the spectacle of locomotives storming Hopton bank certainly belongs to a past age.

Expresses through the Peak

Half way between Manchester and Sheffield lies Edale, a tiny settlement nestling below the inhospitable waste of Kinder Scout. The Pennine Way begins here and many hikers pause at Grindslow Knoll high above the village to gaze back at a grand panorama of the Vale of Edale with Mam Tor beyond. Some may even catch a glimpse of one of the few St Pancras to Manchester trains making its way along the distant railway and remark how minute it seems in comparison with the sweeping fells. Such expresses are relative newcomers to these wild moors however, for until 1968 they crossed the Derbyshire hills between Ambergate and Chinley by an even more spectacular route via Miller's Dale. Now that this line has been closed north of Matlock, one of the most beautiful railway journeys in Britain is no longer possible.

In 1849 a modest branch was opened from the North Midland line at Ambergate to Rowsley, a village in the Derwent Valley south of Chatsworth Park. Though the Manchester, Buxton, Matlock & Midland Junction Railway, as this concern pompously called itself, made no further progress towards realising its ambitions, both the Midland and LNWR managements showed immediate interest in its $11\frac{1}{2}$ miles of track. Whereas the former conjured up visions of a main line to Manchester, the latter naturally wished to thwart such a scheme in order to safeguard its own interests.

Both giants bought shares in the little railway and from 1852 they leased it jointly. Nevertheless, the Midland pressed ahead with its plans and secured parliamentary approval for the Rowsley to Buxton and Miller's Dale to New Mills lines together with running powers to allow expresses to reach the cotton capital. But there remained the possibility that the MBM & MJ would sell out to the LNWR, so an alternative springing point for the Manchester route was established in the form of the Wirksworth branch, completed in 1867. Happily for the Midland, they succeeded in purchasing the Rowsley line outright during 1871.

Construction work through the Peak District proved a difficult and costly business. Had not the Duke of Devonshire been so appalled by the thought of steam engines running through Chatsworth Park, the main line would almost certainly have followed the Derwent Valley to Bamford before assuming a course similar to the present route through Edale. But because of his opposition the Midland was obliged to branch from the MBM & MJ just short of its northern terminus and strike westwards along the Wye Valley, a daunting prospect in view of the difficult country ahead.

Beyond Rowsley the valley sides begin to close in and the Midland veered away from the river to gain height. A tunnel carried the tracks under Monsal Head but where they emerged from its western portal there began a superbly engineered stretch of mountain railway. Much of the neighbouring countryside consisted of rolling uplands, but the line shunned these and followed the River Wye where it had carved a sinuous gorge deep into the limestone hills. Landslides, tough rock and abrupt changes in topography caused the engineers numerous headaches while work on the line was in progress, but once trains had started to operate, passengers were treated to some delightful scenery, especially in the narrow confines of Monsal Dale, Miller's Dale and Chee Dale where the sparkling river flowed over a rocky bed.

The metals clung to the precipitous valley sides by an artificial ledge carved high above the river, but tunnels were required through the rocky shoulders which stood in the way and two viaducts had to be built: a grand stone structure at

Monsal Head and a lofty iron affair at Miller's Dale. One of the finest views of the railway is to be had from the hillside above the former (184715). Generations of expresses have made their way along this beautiful valley: from crimson lake Midland engines with trains of clerestory-roofed coaches to modern diesels with rolling stock painted in blue and grey. The journey was never a particularly rapid one for gradients as severe as 1 in 90 combined with the unavoidable curves prevented fast running. Passengers had every opportunity to enjoy the delights of the Wye Valley, and only those unmoved by one of the loveliest parts of England failed to look out of the carriage window.

Perhaps observant travellers noticed that most of the station buildings were splendid creations too. The Midland spent a lot of money on the architecture for this line, partly because they wanted to make an impression with their new route to Manchester, but also for the approval of the aristocracy whose country houses were particularly abundant in this area of Derbyshire. Bakewell and Hassop stations, together with the new facilities at Rowsley, incorporated sizeable structures which were solidly built in stone and possessed typical Midland gabled canopies. Some very fine carved stonework was to be found facing the platforms, including columns with foliated capitals and peculiar shields flanked by sprays of leaves which varied with each station. Rowsley was notable for its subway, Bakewell for its inconvenient site high above the town, and Hassop for its remote position in the midst of open farmland.

Great Longstone station was very different (page 106). It displayed Midland architecture at its best, for the compact stone building had exceptionally steeply-pitched roofs capped by decorative ridge tiles, splendid bargeboards rich in tracery, and ornate finials at each apex. The chimneys were tall and elegant, there was an interesting little dormer window, and even the platform shelter boasted its share of carved woodwork. Darley Dale station showed a different interpretation of the gothic style. It too consisted of tall buildings with steep roofs, but the local stone had become black with grime which gave the place a sombre, almost forbidding appearance. The gaunt chimneys and pointed arches made it one of the most truly gothic of all Midland stations.

The original Rowsley terminus of the MBM & MJ served as goods offices until recently and consequently remained in a reasonable state of repair. It was a single-storey stone building with round-arched windows and a low roof, the wide eaves of which were supported on wooden brackets. In contrast, Miller's Dale was a comparatively modern station, having been rebuilt during the construction of the duplicate lines in 1905. The main structures followed Midland practice for the period and were of orange stone.

Taken together, the railway buildings between Matlock and Buxton displayed the finest selection of station architecture in the East Midlands. But now the tracks have gone and only a line of ballast threads through the Wye gorge. The poet Ruskin, whose condemnation of the railway that spoilt his beloved valley is often quoted, would no doubt find it incredible that Monsal Dale viaduct has been declared of historical and architectural interest. The time has passed when a Buxton fool might find himself in Bakewell and a Bakewell fool in Buxton at the end of twelve minutes, at least if he contemplates travelling by train. The railway which dragged its close-clinging damnation into each cleft, dingle and wooded hollow has become redundant and steam locomotives no longer shake the hillsides nor cast trails of white smoke across limestone crags (page 103).

The Tissington Trail

At Mapleton Lane near Ashbourne a motorist may park his car and amble along a pleasant footpath called the Tissington Trail (176469). If energetic enough he can walk for twelve miles through a lonely and beautiful part of Derbyshire, gradually climbing from the well-wooded Bradbourne Valley to a windy part of the limestone uplands above Dovedale.

During his stroll it must occur to the least observant visitor that the strong girder bridges and substantial embankments he encounters were built to carry something heavier than pedestrians. In fact, this delightful walk follows part of the LNWR Ashbourne to Buxton railway which was opened in 1899. It was a line with a beauty and fascination all of its own. Even the stations had romantic sounding names: Thorpe Cloud; Parsley Hay; Alsop en le Dale; Tissington.

In retrospect, to construct a railway through this undulating and sparsely settled terrain seems a reckless and extravagant act, but during the 1890s there were perfectly good reasons to justify the expense. Then, as now, expresses between Manchester and London travelled either through Crewe or via Stoke-on-Trent. The LNWR saw that if they were to lay rails from Stockport through Whaley Bridge, Buxton and Ashbourne to Lichfield an alternative and possibly shorter main line between the two cities would be created. Such a route would capture Buxton traffic from the Midland, open up some charming countryside to tourists, and enable milk from the area to reach London more quickly. It was an encouraging prospect, especially as the line north of Buxton had already been built.

That was the dream; a start was made on turning it into reality by obtaining an Act for the Buxton to Ashbourne section. Exactly nine years elapsed and £1½ million was spent before this steeply graded, tightly curved and heavily engineered line was completed. Although every bridge was designed to accommodate double track, no doubt with grand visions of Euston expresses in mind, much of the route carried but one set of rails with passing loops at each station. The Buxton to Parsley Hay section, some of which had been rebuilt from the C & HPR, first carried passengers in 1894, but it was another five years before services were extended to Ashbourne. There the enterprise foundered. To use the railway for fast traffic was out of the question for northbound trains faced a tortuous climb of 900ft in 17 miles, mostly at a gradient of 1 in 60, to reach the summit 1,250ft above sea level.

Structural work on the line was impressive. A tunnel was bored under Ashbourne and another pierced a limestone knoll near Hindlow; Buxton itself was straddled by a high viaduct and one of even loftier construction strode across Duke's Drive south of the town. It is rumoured that the skeletons of men who had been trapped in old mine workings were unearthed when foundations for Hand Dale viaduct at Hartington were being dug. Rock cuttings were numerous, the largest being that at Coldeaton where an excavation $\frac{3}{4}$ mile long and 60ft deep was created with the aid of 200 navvies and 8 steam cranes (160575).

In marked contrast to its rugged earthworks the branch possessed decidedly flimsy stations built of timber. Even the platforms consisted of wooden planking supported on trestles. Accommodation at Alsop en le Dale and Thorpe Cloud was in wooden huts, whereas the other stations at least provided canopies and were of a less frugal design, their size varying according to the settlement served. Though far from opulent, the LNWR buildings were not unattractive and towards the end, after years of disuse and decay, they acquired a forlorn look which was undoubtedly emphasised by their surroundings. Tissington station hid in a wooded cutting near the village, while Hartington station lay $1\frac{1}{2}$ miles uphill from its settlement and reared starkly above the road on an embankment. Here, the view of the Dove Valley was superb and ahead the railway snaked around the hillside, slicing through protruding spurs in grey cuttings. An even finer view, over to Peak Forest and Kinder Scout, was to be had from Hindlow, though the station itself was dominated by massive quarries and belching lime kilns. Bleakest of all was Parsley Hay, isolated and without shelter on a windy limestone plateau with pale green pastures, odd clumps of trees and drystone walls stretching away for miles.

Ashbourne, however, enjoyed the most extensive passenger facilities (page 106). In 1852 the town had heartily celebrated the opening of a North Staffordshire Railway branch from Rocester, but when the LNWR line was built the stately old brick and stone terminus became part of the goods depot (175461), and a new station to allow for through working was constructed further north (177463). The second station was almost entirely wooden; horizontal boarding completed the buildings, platforms consisted of planking which became treacherous when wet, and a canopy curving gracefully with the tracks was extended over the double gates through which passengers could enter from the street. Before Ashbourne station was opened, scores of navvies slept there after an arduous day working on the line.

Before passenger services were withdrawn from the branch in 1954, a typical Buxton North Western to Uttoxeter train consisted of an LMS 2-6-4 tank hauling a couple of non-corridor coaches. Even in its more prosperous days the line saw only six local trains in each direction daily, and the forecasted alternative route from Manchester to London materialised as two through carriages each way between Euston and Buxton via Burton, Ashby and Nuneaton.

Nevertheless the villagers appreciated their railway. A few days before the line opened a free excursion ran to Ashbourne for the folk of Hartington, many of whom had never experienced a train journey, and when the weather was exceptionally bad the branch became almost a lifeline. In really severe winters such places as Hartington were cut off for days by snowdrifts, but somehow the trains managed to get through. When ordinary services were closed down, local people demanded, and received, an assurance that emergency winter services would be retained. These were eventually discontinued in 1963, though they had proved their worth that very year when essential supplies were brought by rail once again. Ramblers' excursions from Manchester, chiefly for the delights of Dovedale and the attractions of the Tissington well-dressing ceremony, came to an end at the same time. Nowadays, the rails north of Hindlow are busy with quarry traffic, but cars and coaches bring the tourists and lorries fetch the milk. A walk along the Tissington Trail allows one ample time to consider whether the LNWR invested its money wisely. Cer-

High Peak contrast: **Plate 13** (above) *an ancient LNWR 'Crewe Goods' grinds round Gotham Curve during the 1880s;* **Plate 14** (below) *41164 and 45616* **Malta GC** *pound through Rowsley with a St Pancras to Manchester express on 12 July 1958, leaving a trail of smoke through the drizzle-soaked hills*

Nottingham Victoria: Plate 15 (above) *the south end of the station from Parliament Street bridge in LNER days, showing a Newcastle to Bournemouth express and various local trains;* Plate 16 (below) *a Grantham to Derby train at platform 1 on 18 June 1960*

tainly one amenity they had no intention of providing was a peaceful footpath away from congested roads and noisy cities.

Along the Amber Valley

LMS expresses taking the North Midland route between Derby and Leeds passed beneath the industrial township of Clay Cross by a lengthy tunnel whose soot-blackened smoke vents stood in a row between the old terraced houses. As their train emerged from the castellated northern portal into a deep cutting, few passengers were aware that a hard-working but picturesque narrow-gauge line lay just above them (396642). The undistinguished Clay Cross terminus of the Ashover Light Railway was overshadowed by blast furnaces, slag banks and workshops associated with the town's ironworks, but these unsavoury surroundings foretold little of the scenic journey to Ashover, $7\frac{1}{2}$ miles and 45 minutes away.

George Stephenson, as engineer to the North Midland, was supervising work on Clay Cross tunnel when an abundance of coal seams was unearthed. He promptly decided to exploit these, so in 1837 the concern which became the Clay Cross Company was founded, and ironworks as well as collieries were soon in production. During 1918 a scheme was put forward for a railway along the Amber Valley to help develop quarries supplying limestone and fluorspar, both of which were vital to ironmaking. Seven years later this project materialised and the 2ft-gauge Ashover Light Railway began operations. Though mineral traffic was slow to develop and most of the limestone that was eventually carried went to main line railways as ballast, the public flocked to travel on the little trains. Passengers had rated low in the initial scale of priorities, but during the first ten years of its life the ALR carried well over a quarter of a million people, most of whom picnicked beside the Amber or dined and danced at the 'Where the Rainbow Ends' cafe which the company built at Ashover Butts (343633).

The hamlet of Dalebank was little more than a couple of

Great Longstone and Ashbourne stations

cottages and the occasional farmhouse, yet it possessed its own station (360616). In common with other ALR halts, the primitive facilities consisted of no more than a small wooden waiting shelter roofed in corrugated iron together with a low ash bank serving as a platform. At Fallgate a similar building still stands, and though somewhat dismal it is worthy of inspection as the only surviving ALR passenger building in situ (355621). Dalebank is a quiet place today. Towards Clay Cross all that remains of the railway is a vague ledge above the stream, while in the Ashover direction only a low hump across the fields and the remains of brick flood arches mark its course. But in 1925, when the station paintwork was fresh and the earthworks still raw, Dalebank was served by a passenger train for the first time. A column of smoke rose above the trees, a whistle echoed round the Amber Valley and the clatter of narrow-gauge carriages drew near.

When the train emerged from the trees it presented a very smart though most unusual appearance. Both locomotive and coaches were painted in deep red lined out in gold: a pleasing contrast to the green hues of their surroundings. The engine was unmistakably American with its tall stovepipe chimney, twin domes, squat pannier tanks and enormous cab. It was one of four purchased from the War Stores Disposals Board and similar to numerous machines which had been built by Baldwins in Philadelphia for service at the western front during World War I. Even the carriages ran on ex-War Department bogies, though their elegant timber bodies had been specially constructed. They followed tramway tradition by having end-balconies, longitudinal wooden seats and leather straps hanging from the ceiling.

The landscape changed from industrial devastation at Clay Cross to pleasant farming country around Stretton, but between Dalebank and Ashover the hills of grit and limestone closed in on the Amber. So constricted was the valley that the railway had to cross and recross the river in order to find suitable flat land for its trackbed. Because of their tiny bogies, the carriages appeared to be travelling fast, but in fact there was ample time to contemplate the steep fields with their dark brown walls, the old toadstone quarries, and the tough-looking little cottages. Initially the line provided a welcome escape for people living in the grimy coalfield towns, but as bus excursions gained favour so the trip by narrow-gauge train became less of a novelty. After 1936 the ALR became a shabby industrial line and when the end came in 1950 its remaining locomotives were worn out and rusty, its wagons decrepit, and its trackbed overgrown. Had construction been delayed for a couple of years the line would probably never have been built for it came as the motor lorry was just beginning to have an effect. As it was, the chairman of the Clay Cross Company arrived for the opening ceremony by car!

CHAPTER 6

City of Nottingham

A Midland Stronghold

Eleven centuries ago Danish settlers established the township of Snotingaham on hilly ground just north of the broad Trent floodplain. Since then Nottingham has spread well beyond its castle set high above the river on a sandstone bluff and now sprawls westwards to Wollaton, eastwards to Gedling and northwards along the Leen Valley to Bulwell. Even the corrugations of Thorneywood and Mapperley failed to prevent streets of Victorian terraces and acres of modern estates from reaching Arnold on the very edge of Sherwood Forest. Though its commercial wealth was initially based on lacemaking, the city is best known today as the home of three famous firms manufacturing cigarettes, pharmaceuticals and bicycles. Equally important is its status as regional centre for coalfield towns to the north and west, and its claim to be Queen of the Midlands is emphasised by proud civic buildings such as the Council House overlooking Old Market Square.

Such an important place was bound to attract the attention of railway builders at an early date. When the Midland Counties Company opened its station at Carrington Street in 1839, the city enjoyed a train service for the first time and was soon in direct communication with London via Leicester and

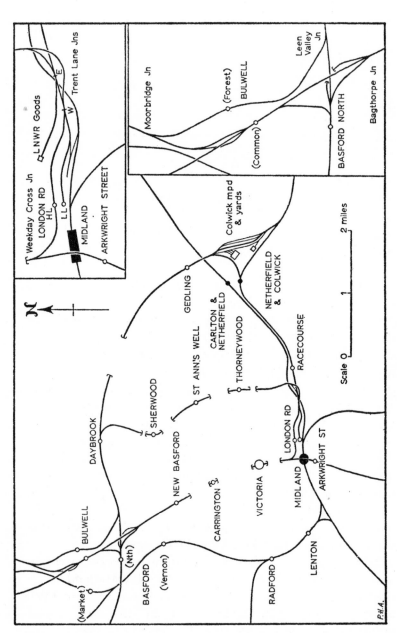

Map of the railways in Nottingham

Rugby. In 1844 this local enterprise became a constituent of the Midland Railway which built lines affording Nottingham access to Lincoln (1846), the Erewash Valley (1847), and Mansfield (1848). Some thirty years later the cut-off between Radford and Trowell was opened, shortly followed by another important line south-eastwards to Melton Mowbray. This formed part of a new route to London and enabled through expresses from the north of England to serve Nottingham without the reversal necessary before 1880. It was a heavily engineered railway and less than a mile from the Midland station it crossed the Trent by a magnificent three-span girder bridge approached on brick arches embellished in the Gothic style.

Thus the Midland's contribution to railways in Nottingham was more or less complete. With the exception of the Mansfield line, where passenger trains no longer run, and the Melton line which has been closed to all normal traffic though still largely intact for testing the Advanced Passenger Train, it is this network which carries present day rail services from the city. But interwoven with these surviving routes there once existed a completely separate system of tracks which were just as busy with main line and suburban traffic in their heyday. Even the present Midland station, a pompous and lavishly decorated affair, was opened during 1904 in response to the freshly completed and fiercely competitive Great Central facilities. Though now almost totally disused, the maze of lines centred on Nottingham Victoria provided some fascinating examples of the extravagant side of the railway age.

The Challenge

A seemingly innocent branch from Grantham turned out to be the first step in an invasion which broke the Midland's monopoly both within Nottingham and throughout the coalfield. In 1850 an over-optimistic company calling itself the Ambergate, Nottingham, Boston & Eastern Junction Railway started to run trains into the city by way of Colwick Junction on the Lincoln line. Although it appeared highly likely that this feeble concern would be absorbed by the Midland, it was the Great Northern which successfully intervened with an agreement over running powers. When its main route through Grantham was brought into use during 1852 the GNR decided to run an express between King's Cross and Nottingham in less time than it took the rival Midland train. This was too much for the Midland, so as soon as the intruder arrived it was surrounded by Midland locomotives and shunted into a disused shed where it remained in captivity for seven months. Tension between the two companies continued until a separate line was opened from Netherfield to a terminus at London Road during 1857. At last the GNR had secured proper access to Nottingham. Though the original junction at Colwick was removed shortly after this, it was reinstated almost a century later enabling Grantham trains to run into Midland station once more.

Having thus obtained a foothold in the East Midlands, the GNR looked greedily at the abundant coal reserves so close at hand. It was with the intention of tapping these that the company proposed a line to Codnor Park in the Erewash Valley, but this scheme met with little success and there began a long and frustrating conflict with the Midland over rates for through coal traffic. In 1872, however, there came a spectacular breakthrough when the Derbyshire Extension Bill was sanctioned by Parliament. This promised to be much more of an invasion than the earlier plan, for not only did it involve a branch to Pinxton in the Erewash Valley, but the main line was to continue westwards through Ilkeston and Derby as far as Burton on Trent.

The new railway, which first carried trains in 1875, described a huge arc round the northern parts of Nottingham and from Netherfield to Basford it was known locally as the 'Back Line'. It began with a sweeping triangular junction at Colwick and from Gedling climbed steadily at 1 in 100 past colliery spoil heaps to a craggy sandstone cutting which prepared the way for Mapperley Plains tunnel. This suffered badly from mining subsidence and in 1925 about 150 tons of rubble completely blocked it when part of the roof collapsed. A procession of heavy freight trains rumbling through it did little to help matters and despite a speed restriction the bore became so unstable that this section of line had to be abandoned abruptly in 1960. From a summit just west of here the tracks descended into Arno Vale and through Daybrook to the Leen Valley.

Much of the route now lies obscured, especially near Arnold where a new housing estate has destroyed almost every trace. Standing in this blissful residential backwater one finds it hard to imagine the ground shaking with the valiant struggles of elderly steam engines as they hauled fully laden trains from Nottinghamshire pits towards Colwick yard. In reality coal traffic over this piece of railway was exceptionally heavy, especially in the afternoon when train after train blasted up to Mapperley Plains. Empty wagons for the collieries and full loads of iron ore for Stanton Ironworks travelled in the opposite direction while a great deal of general goods traffic came this way too.

The Back Line was built primarily for moving coal but its passenger services were even more interesting. Until alternatives became available it carried all GNR trains to the north or west, and as late as 1939 there were nine trains in each direction on the celebrated outer circle service between Nottingham and Basford. Most workings consisted of non-corridor coaches hauled by an engine from Colwick shed, though at one time an LNER steam railcar provided a couple of the off-peak services. Road competition inevitably captured much of this traffic and when the few remaining journeys were suddenly cancelled in 1960 a substitute bus service called at the stations for some months. Colliers' trains once ran to Gedling where a special wooden platform was provided near the mine, and holiday trains stopping at local stations from Derby or Pinxton travelled this way to avoid Nottingham itself.

Precious little now remains of this extremely busy railway. Some people may express curiosity at the strange brick smoke vent on Mapperley Plains while others may have memories of the crowded platform at Daybrook prior to the arrival of a Skegness excursion. At least the large brick buildings of Gedling station still overlook the beautiful bowed spire of the parish church. They are typical of those on the original Derbyshire Extension and have been attractively modified as a youth centre.

Colwick

As GNR metals began to spread through the colliery district it became obvious that new marshalling yards together with a larger locomotive shed would be essential, for the limited facilities at London Road were not capable of dealing with the rapidly increasing coal traffic. An admirable site was selected at Colwick where the Derbyshire Extension began and where ample flat land existed.

During 1879 both Colwick yard and the first part of the motive power depot were brought into use. However, when more branch lines were opened north of Nottingham the original four-road shed proved inadequate and a massive structure covering eight tracks was built to house the swelling stud of engines. Even then, a further four-road shed was erected early this century. Besides accommodation for the locomotives themselves there were repair shops, stores, mess rooms and a whole range of offices necessary to organise and run such a vast complex. A separate shed was built by the LNWR for working its own trains over the joint line through High Leicestershire, and near its site remains a row of houses rejoicing in the name London North Western Terrace (628405). Netherfield itself became a miniature railway community but it has outlived the huge sheds on which it was once so dependent.

At one time the locomotive fleet at Colwick reached as many as 400. There were row upon row of them: some gently simmering, others smoking profusely, several blowing off steam in readiness for work, a few rusting and awaiting repair. An army of 0–6–0 tanks was needed to shunt the yards and haul local goods trains, while passenger services around Nottingham and throughout the coalfield required more sprightly engines. At first, Stirling 2–4–0 tender and 0–4–4 tank locomotives served this purpose, but by the 1920s they were being displaced by newer Ivatt 4–4–0s and 4–4–2 tanks which in turn succumbed to modern 0–6–2, 2–6–0 and 4–6–0 types. The larger engines also proved particularly useful on seaside excursion trains. Coal was brought from the pithead to Colwick by generations of 0–6–0 tender locomotives, though these frequently found employment on passenger duties too. Until the early 1930s one of the hefty Ivatt 0–8–2 tanks could be seen struggling to the marshalling yards with loaded wagons which were then sorted and dispatched to London or the Eastern Counties in complete trains with an Ivatt 'Long Tom' 0–8–0 in charge. More recently this traffic was handled by powerful 2–8–0s.

The sheds functioned round the clock every day of the year, and for much of the time clanking buffers or shrill whistles indicated activity in the adjoining yards. If a damp mist drifted in from the Trent as several engines were being stoked up a sulphurous yellow smog hung over Colwick with only the occasional cough and curse to punctuate the oppressive murk. Crews wearing blue overalls and peaked caps arrived on duty carrying their 'snap' tins containing essential sustenance, visited the running foreman's office to ascertain the number and location of their charge, then checked duty rosters and notice boards. In the adjacent offices clerks sat at high desks to deal with engine repair cards or staff record sheets in copper-plate writing and occasionally dreamed of the day when promotion would arrive.

But with the slackening demand for coal, the advent of diesel locomotives and the closure of most former GNR branches in the district, Colwick depot became redundant. The mighty steel and concrete coal tower which had stood as a 70ft high landmark since its installation in 1938 was felled by explosives on 29 December 1971. Inside the silent sheds the ground was thick with sticky grease and an acrid tang still hung in the air, from soot-caked walls and girders. The place was a heartbreaking shambles to those who remembered it when it never slept; now it lives in the memory alone.

The Suburban Railway

Within the residential inner suburbs of eastern Nottingham lie traces of the overgrown earthworks and redundant tunnels which once carried a double-track railway between the Grantham line at Trent Lane Junction and Daybrook on the Derbyshire Extension. But the course of the erstwhile Nottingham Suburban Railway is far from continuous, for such is the pressure on land in this part of the city that the former track bed has been extensively re-developed.

The company obtained its Act during 1886 and within three and a half years construction work was completed. Though worked as part of the Great Northern system for 55 per cent of its gross earnings, this small concern remained independent until it was absorbed by the LNER in 1923. Unfortunately the line became more or less superfluous only seven years after it opened, and though in retrospect it must be judged as a misguided piece of enterprise, it would be unfair to suggest that the group of local businessmen who promoted it totally lacked foresight for in 1886 there were convincing arguments for its construction.

GNR passenger trains from Nottingham to such towns as Ilkeston and Derby had to make a lengthy detour through Gedling before heading west. Besides providing an alternative to this congested route, the Nottingham Suburban Railway would shorten the through journey by nearly three miles as well as stimulate residential and industrial traffic. So the prospects were good, and a healthy future seemed in store. But even as the inaugural train climbed away from Trent Lane, construction work was in progress on the Manchester, Sheffield & Lincolnshire line to Annesley. By 1900 this new railway had been extended through Nottingham itself and as it provided the GNR with an even more convenient route to the west the majority of local services were diverted on to it. Overnight the Suburban route had lost its *raison d'etre* and, furthermore, what few customers its three stations had managed to attract were soon tempted away by electric trams which began to serve Sherwood in 1901. Freight traffic fared somewhat better as three brickworks installed connections with the railway and the remains of two such branches are still to be seen near Thorneywood and Sherwood stations.

Considering its meagre achievements, the $3\frac{3}{4}$ mile line was a very costly venture. Land itself was inexpensive and most of the £$\frac{1}{4}$ million was spent on conquering the undulating terrain around Mapperley with 1,048yd of tunnelling, numerous embankments and cuttings, and a dozen or more substantial bridges such as the high brick arch which still spans Thackeray's Lane (582442). Bold but elegant structural work executed in hard blue brick was a characteristic of the Nottingham Suburban Railway, and other fine examples which remain are the portals of Ashwell's tunnel, the retaining wall at Thorneywood station and the overbridge at Sherwood station.

Though a journey over the line lasted but a few minutes, it was one involving arduous work for the locomotive and constantly changing prospects for the passenger. At Trent Lane Junction, trains heading north rose steeply away from the Grantham tracks on a sharp curve while those returning to London Road had first to cross the GNR on a pair of large bowstring spans. These two single-line spurs converged beyond a split-level plate girder bridge over the Midland's Lincoln branch and climbed continuously up to Sherwood Tunnel, over 200ft higher.

Each of the three stations lay in its own little valley and was provided with side platforms of considerable length and breadth in anticipation of the daily rush which failed to materialise. Their red brick buildings were reminiscent of contemporary GNR practice as far as the tall, bulbous chimneys, low-pitched slate roofs and wooden canopies supported on cast iron brackets were concerned, but they had more than their share of ornamental work as is illustrated by each of the surviving station houses at Thorneywood and St Ann's Well.

Initially the passenger service was an optimistic one of ten northbound and nine southbound trains daily, most of them being hauled by diminutive GNR Stirling 0–4–4 tanks which experienced considerable difficulty in starting trains on the gradients when the rails were greasy. They made a splendid sight with a rake of varnished teak carriages, whether easing through the mist towards Trent Lane Junction or attacking the 1 in 50 bank up to Sherwood tunnel on a summer afternoon. No doubt many gardeners have paused from working on their allotments to watch a train struggle up from St Ann's Well and gradually disappear into the deep cutting gouged out of the rising valley floor.

But there were few passengers to appreciate the aesthetics of either train or station and the Nottingham Suburban Railway stopping service was abandoned in 1916 as a war-time economy measure. At the same time the through service was reduced to two trains only from Nottingham to Shirebrook. In 1930 the track was singled, after which a solitary afternoon train bound for the Leen Valley behind an Ivatt 4–4–2 tank made the journey up to Sherwood. When this was withdrawn in 1931 a pick-up goods ran between Daybrook and Thorneywood, though the section south of here became disused, which was just as well for a bomb destroyed part of the embankment near Colwick Road during a 1941 air raid. For much of its existence the Nottingham Suburban Railway had been an embarrassment rather than an asset to all who were responsible for it, and the lingering death which began in 1900 finally came 51 years later. Now there are blocks of flats on two of its station sites and the mysterious tunnel mouths and weed-choked cuttings provide an adventure playground for a generation which knows little of this ill-fated railway (page 138).

An Upheaval

At a time when the Nottingham Suburban Railway was still

young and hopefully striving to develop its traffic, Parliament sanctioned the most expensive section of railway the East Midlands has known and one which drastically altered large parts of urban Nottingham. When planning their London Extension, the Manchester, Sheffield & Lincolnshire Railway decided to strike a path through the heart of the city and combine with the Great Northern to provide an impressive new station which would put the rival Midland facilities to shame. After colossal expenditure the culmination of this grandiose scheme came in 1900 when Nottingham Victoria handled passenger trains for the first time and the Great Central Railway, as the MS & L had more appropriately become, was fully established in the city. The Queen of the Midlands had acquired her finest main line yet and a superb central station into the bargain.

Southbound trains swept down to the city through Bulwell where they crossed the Leen Valley, but steadily rising ground lay ahead and beyond Basford the railway plunged into Sherwood Rise and Mansfield Road tunnels. Because of the houses above, the latter was devoid of ventilation shafts and frequently became very foul, especially as heavy trains leaving Nottingham had to hammer through it on a rising gradient of 1 in 130. Immediately beyond its southern portal the tracks fanned out through Victoria station, only to converge and disappear underground once more at the other end of the platforms.

Unlike those to the north, which were driven through solid sandstone, Victoria Street tunnel lay very close to the surface and was formed by the cut-and-cover method along the line of Thurland Street. During construction work the cellars of several buildings actually collapsed, and when navvies broke through the beer store of Cross Keys Inn the landlord found his stocks more than a little depleted! At Weekday Cross, where the ground rapidly fell away and the railway emerged from underneath the Lace Market into a short cutting, some rock cells complete with iron shackles and the remains of prisoners were excavated below the site of the old town hall.

Ahead lay the Marsh, a low-lying area occupied by acres of festering slums through which the Great Central thrust a long and complicated viaduct, the most spectacular part of which was a 170ft long bowstring span over the Midland station. Only the Trent itself then stood as an obstacle to progress southwards into Leicestershire, but three pairs of 112ft lattice girders were needed to carry the quadruple track across it.

By participating in the erection of Victoria station, the Great Northern was rescued from its remote premises in London Road and built a series of connections which afforded access to the new line. The most substantial of these ran from Trent Lane Junction to Weekday Cross and negotiated a part of the city already crowded with factories, store yards, streets and canals. A great deal of money had to be spent both on the land required for a path through this congested area and on the viaduct along which most of the line was carried. For some distance the tracks ran on a steel trestle which straddled the gasworks sidings, though even more impressive was a massive lattice deck girder structure spanning the junction of two canals. Besides the rails themselves, it supported part of a new passenger station which virtually replaced the adjoining terminus.

Nottingham possessed no less than twenty-six stations within 2½ miles of the city centre and of these London Road High Level enjoyed the least attractive surroundings. The viaduct widened to accommodate a gently curving island platform which stood high above the canal but was nevertheless dominated by huge factories and stark gasometers. On it were erected a series of wooden buildings with intricate panelling and plenty of windows in small square panes, while a gabled glass roof and canopy supported on cast iron columns with lattice-work spandrels provided the necessary shelter. Access was by means of a railed-in staircase that ascended from the subway and booking hall, both of which were finished in brown and cream glazed bricks. The street-level building was a dull affair in red brick, though its ribbed chimneys and recessed facade incorporating both window and doorway in one unit were characteristically Great Northern.

Fascinating as it was in terms of layout and setting, High Level station paled architecturally in comparison with the grand old Low Level terminus which faced it across a fore-court and service road. Though similarly constructed in red brick, the earlier building had an immensely complex front-age incorporating ample and vigorous stone embellishments such as balustrades, cornices and dripstones. Ornate gables and parapets were decorated with diaper patterning, the roof was crowned by a truncated spire capped with ornamental railings, and a projecting *porte-cochere* provided cover for waiting road carriages. In 1900 High Level station inherited almost all GNR services previously handled by the spacious terminus, though the trains to Northampton via High Leice-stershire still started from there until 1944. These of course were the responsibility of the LNWR at the turn of the century, and that company had failed to secure running powers into Victoria.

But it was the new station that bustled with factory and office workers during weekday rush hours. Even after the Surburban Railway, Leen Valley and Basford services had been curtailed, its dingy slumber was punctuated by short bursts of activity as the Grantham line trains came and went. When these were diverted into Nottingham Midland during 1967 the High Level, which by then reeked of decay, finally shut up shop. Its maroon and cream paint was beginning to peel; the glass which had not been smashed was thick with dust; and the board advising passengers to alight for Trent Bridge cricket and football grounds had long disappeared. With its veneer of industrial grime, its dank and gloomy sub-way and its distinctive odour formed from the blended aromas of canal and gasworks, the place had a character all of its own (page 137).

More connections between the GCR and GNR systems were installed some three miles north of Victoria where the new main line intersected the Derbyshire Extension. At Basford the layout involved three levels and meant that GNR trains from Derby and Pinxton direct to Victoria had to drive through a short, curving tunnel known affectionately as the 'rat hole'. Beyond Bulwell another link enabled the GCR to reach Leen Valley metals, though it was also used by certain Shirebrook passenger workings. The area is now totally devoid of track and the complicated layout will shortly be covered by redevelopment.

Arkwright Street station stood alongside the GCR main line south of Weekday Cross and in several respects it resembled London Road High Level which lay half a mile away across the city. It was similarly perched on a viaduct amid grim surroundings, though these consisted of gaunt three-storey terraced houses rather than industrial properties. The place had a most gruesome appearance from below for the brick viaduct was flanked by ugly girder structures supporting each of the side platforms. A cramped doorway in the abutment of Waterway Street bridge and a slightly larger entrance in Arkwright Street itself gave access to a tall booking hall finished in cream glazed bricks. As this dismal room was squashed between the viaduct arches and a back lane it required one rectangular and two octagonal skylights for the necessary illumination. Even more gloomy were the staircases that rose to a couple of little brick pavilions giving access to the north end of each platform.

In contrast to this cramped approach the platforms themselves were quite spacious and clearly designed to cope with peak-hour crowds; they proved especially useful during 1899 when Arkwright Street became the principal GCR station in Nottingham pending the completion of Victoria. Buildings at this height were of lightweight timber construction and set back enough to require a separate framework from ground level. Those on the west side were larger and passengers travelling into Nottingham had the added benefit of a lengthy but austere canopy. Particularly curious were two metal chutes spiralling down from this side of the station to an alley below. While most of the city slept they performed a vital service, for each morning a newspaper train drew into Arkwright Street and its contents had to be speedily transferred to waiting vans in good time for early deliveries.

Passengers aboard a train approaching Nottingham from the south enjoyed a superb panorama of the city rising away beyond the rooftops of Broadmarsh, and this sight could be quite breathtaking when familiar landmarks were silhouetted against an evening sky. But the occupants of the miserable dwellings overshadowed by Arkwright Street station were hardly appreciative of this spectacle, for the platforms were at roof level and only a matter of yards away from their windows. As far as the amount of noise, the lack of daylight and privacy, and the sheer ugliness of their environment were concerned, these were the unhappiest properties in the city.

Just as it had deputised for Victoria at the turn of the century, Arkwright Street gained a new lease of life when that great station closed its barriers for the last time in 1967. It had been disused for over four years, but with a coat of paint and a new sign over the entrance the ageing buildings and platform on the east side became a terminus for trains from Rugby Central. But this was never intended to be a permanent arrangement and within two years the diesel railcar service was withdrawn leaving Arkwright Street quietly to decay once more.

Carrington was the only other original station on the whole London Extension to have side platforms and, again in common with Arkwright Street, it served a residential part of the city, albeit a more prosperous one. But rather than standing high above the streets it was set in a tremendous sandstone cutting with its platforms extending between the portals of Mansfield Road and Sherwood Rise tunnels. Had it not been for Carrington station the railway would still have been underground here (page 137). The booking office and an adjoining house were at street level and though built largely of red brick they had a somewhat pretentious veneer of tiles and mock-Tudor tack-timbering as well as fussy bargeboards. A long path led to the platforms, each of which was provided with a single-storey building displaying the more familiar

Jacobean touches.

For a few years the station did a reasonable amount of trade though this would have been considerably greater had the electric trams not served the same area. But custom had become negligible by 1929 and Carrington lost its passenger trains. Part of the booking office has found employment as a shop whereas the remainder, of all the unlikely adaptations, now serves as a poodle parlour! In marked contrast to the beauty treatment dispensed therein, the huge cutting stands as a gaping ruin waiting to be filled with rubble and refuse.

A Superb and Central Station

As future generations of shoppers arrive at the Victoria Centre in Nottingham they will have no concept of the vast and busy railway station which once occupied the site. Perhaps one or two will stare at the strange clock tower now dwarfed by concrete skyscrapers and marvel at its ornate balconies or the splendid dome and cupola. Apart from this solitary memorial, nothing remains of what was the grandest station in the East Midlands and one of the finest buildings of its type in all England.

Nottingham Victoria was opened on 24 May 1900. It occupied a superbly convenient site in the centre of the city but meant the acquisition of valuable land and the demolition of considerable property including 1,300 dwellings and 20 public houses. However, much of the area was a decaying slum and its loss to the city was hardly tragic, especially as the GCR was required to build replacement property elsewhere. Eventually the GCR and GNR spent well over £1 million on their joint station: a staggering sum for those days.

Throughout its existence Victoria never failed to impress travellers with its vast dimensions and lavish accommodation. Basically it consisted of two great island platforms nearly a quarter of a mile in length set in a sandstone cutting below street level. In addition there were bays at both ends of each island for local trains, making twelve platforms in all. Loops at either side of the station allowed slow freight trains to wait while expresses overtook them, and surplus carriages could be temporarily stabled on a siding between the centre through lines. Four signal boxes were necessary, but the double-track tunnels at either end of the station were a severe bottleneck for many years.

No expense was spared on the architectural details. The main structure facing Mansfield Road was elegantly designed in the Jacobean style common to the whole London Extension, and employed bright red bricks relieved with cream stone dressings (page 126). Its centrepiece was the imposing tower which stood as a Nottingham landmark and a proud monument to the age of steam. Each island platform possessed two great blocks of buildings which were faced entirely in glazed yellow bricks and terracotta. Besides spacious waiting rooms, vast lavatories and numerous offices they housed two of the signal boxes, a dining room, first and third class refreshment rooms and even a ladies' tea room. The whole central section of the station was covered by a lofty glass roof carried on steel columns. It was indeed a magnificent place!

Though there were local services on the GCR lines out of Victoria, notably the commuter trains to Leicester, Chesterfield and eventually Mansfield, fast trains were of far greater significance. Most important were the heavily used and punctual expresses between Manchester and Marylebone, though the through workings from north-east to south-west England introduced the green coaches of the Southern Railway as well as brown and cream Great Western Railway carriages to the East Midlands. It was possible to step on a train at Victoria and alight at Swansea, Bournemouth, York or Newcastle, and at one time there was even a through carriage between Penzance and Aberdeen! (page 104).

Apart from seasonal excursions and a short-lived Pullman service between Sheffield and King's Cross during early LNER days, operations on the GNR lines around Nottingham were entirely local in character. Before the Grouping, trains of teak coaches hauled by bright green locomotives ran to Grantham,

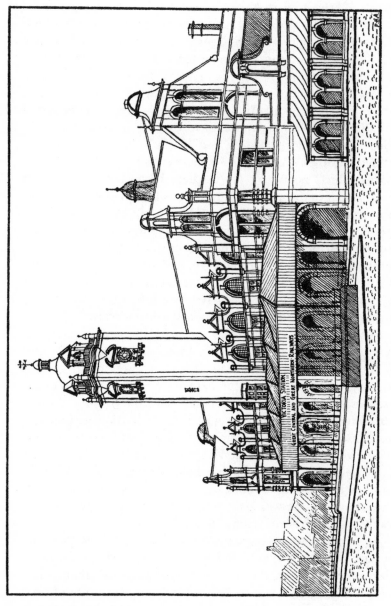

Nottingham Victoria station, exterior

Newark, Basford, Shirebrook, Pinxton, Heanor, Derby and Stafford, advertising their destination by a headboard on the front of the engine not unlike present-day bus services.

But these were bounteous days. After sixty years of industrious service the great station had lost some of its excellence, though not its grandeur, for the remaining roof glass was virtually opaque with soot and the glazed bricks had gathered a mantle of grey dirt. On humid summer afternoons a smoke haze hung over the platforms and the air reeked of steam and hot oil from simmering engines. Groups of small boys fidgeted with notepads and spotter's books as a work-soiled 2–8–0 clanked by with wagons of tawny iron ore for Staveley blast furnaces. Suddenly excited attention was directed towards a fine LNER Pacific guiding the carriages of a Manchester express out of Victoria Street tunnel and across the pointwork towards platform four. Meanwhile, a stopping train to Leicester stood in platform twelve behind a less distinguished 2–6–4 tank and one or two passengers chose their compartment, slammed the door and settled in the faded red upholstery. A few gazed at the watercolour prints on the opposite partition and mused at the contrast between those far-off seaside towns and the drab world outside their carriage window as the express rolled away, its bogies clattering over the rail joints and echoing beneath the station roof.

Nottingham Victoria never recovered from its state of indifferent maintenance. Like the whole London Extension it had become an expensive and unnecessary burden to the diminishing rail network, so its demotion and eventual abandonment were inevitable. Just before its closure, the superfluous giant seemed a desperately lonely and cavernous place. Its sumptuous refreshment rooms lay deep in dust and the broad stairways which once coped with the largest Goose Fair crowds echoed only the occasional footstep. A few mineral trains still rumbled past the empty platforms and now and then the rasping exhaust of a Rugby-bound diesel railcar disturbed the pigeons.

Demolition was swift once the opportunity arose. It was an

odd experience to walk through Victoria Street tunnel and emerge from its blue-brick portal into a half-completed basement of the Victoria Centre. Without question this new enterprise is cleaner than the old station. It might even prove to be as useful. But it will never possess quite the same character, never change its mood with the weather or the time of day and certainly never generate the same nostalgia when it becomes obsolete.

CHAPTER 7

North and West of Nottingham

An Industrial Setting

Nottingham lies just outside the southern fringe of Britain's largest coalfield and beyond the city a populous mining district stretches away towards Mansfield and Chesterfield. Though attempts to improve it are gaining momentum, the landscape in this part of the East Midlands continues to be dominated by the less agreeable by-products of the industrial revolution. Even today there are acres of blackened grass interspersed with pools of stagnant water, while huge spoil tips still rise starkly above colliers' terraces and provide a backcloth to the haphazard array of mining villages and small towns.

Railways still play a vital role in moving coal from the pitheads, but in the past they were very much more a part of the everyday scene. Rows of wagons stood disconsolately on every skyline; tracks seemed to run in all directions; sidings veered away from the main lines and ran over, under or alongside them, only to converge again in tangled junctions. Even in summer, thick palls of smoke took away much of the sunlight, but on a dismal winter afternoon the gloom could be oppressive. Through the murk, trails of steam marked the progress of engines struggling with loaded coal wagons or

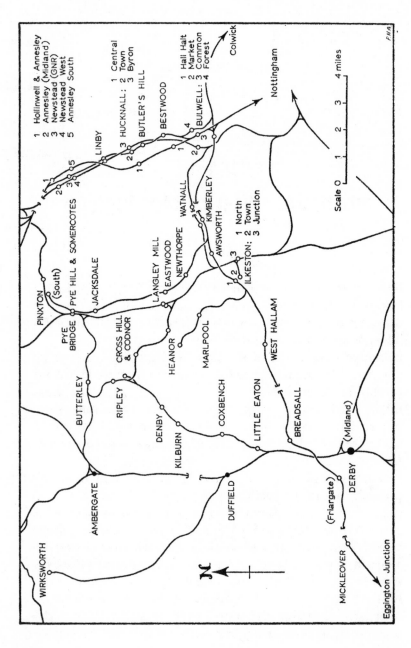

Map of the railways north and west of Nottingham

guiding local passenger trains from one grimy little station to the next; even expresses clattered by with caution for the permanent way had been badly warped by mining subsidence. Shrieking whistles accompanied the clanking of trucks being shunted in colliery sidings and the rumble of heavy trains bound for marshalling yards or steel works echoed round the valleys. Day or night, the activity was ceaseless. It was a region of intense character and the railways were so much a part of it. Improved amenities are obviously necessary, but progress is eroding this distinctive atmosphere and the network of steel rails which represented so much investment has shrunken to a shadow of its former self.

The Midland Under Pressure

During the late eighteenth and early nineteenth centuries a large number of primitive waggonways were built to carry coal from individual pits to wharves alongside the Cromford, Erewash, Nutbrook and Nottingham canals. But with the arrival of the North Midland, Erewash Valley and Nottingham to Mansfield railways in the 1840s, a much more efficient system of communication was established and the Midland acquired a virtual monopoly of south Derbyshire and Nottinghamshire mineral traffic which it was to enjoy for some thirty years. Once the Great Northern and eventually Great Central had gained access to the area, however, an even more intricate web of tracks came to be laid on a landscape which was becoming increasingly industrialised. The new lines immediately entered into direct competition with the existing routes and in retaliation the Midland constructed further branches which were intended to challenge the GNR's successful Derbyshire extension. Both physically and historically the development of the railway network in this area became very complicated indeed.

Having established its three main north to south lines during the 1840s, the Midland did little to expand its interests in the district for several years. Then in 1856 a branch was built from the North Midland line near Little Eaton to Rip-ley, an old market town that had grown substantially with the expansion of mining. This railway passed through a long-established colliery district and ran parallel with the Little Eaton Gangroad, a horse-operated plateway which had opened in 1795, primarily to convey coal to the Derby Canal.

As far as Coxbench the Midland tracks passed through picturesque rural country, but north of here the landscape had been mutilated by mining. Even the stations reflected this change and it is interesting to compare the delightful building at Coxbench with the mean and harsh affair at Denby. Ordin-ary passenger services along the branch were curtailed in 1930, but coal traffic continued and much of this route is still used for this purpose. Between Denby and Ripley however the tracks have been lifted and in places the old formation can scarcely be traced. Local trains bound for Derby originally started at a remote terminus on the outskirts of Ripley (405496), but when the line was extended northwards to Butterley during the 1890s a more central station was built to serve the town, and this is described later.

Once the GNR Derbyshire Extension lines became estab-lished they captured a large share of local passenger business as well as colliery traffic, and the Midland was shaken out of its complacency. Ilkeston, by virtue of its hilltop site over-looking the River Erewash, was one of the larger places served directly by the GNR but not by its rival. The town had been linked with the Erewash Valley route by a rather half-hearted branch line, but this closed to passengers in 1870 and it was another nine years before the service was reinstated, this time with proper station facilities at Ilkeston (465425).

It was far from an attractive journey, for trains leaving the terminus rolled steadily downhill past industrial establish-ments and then crossed the River Erewash and its adjacent canal before reaching a triangular junction with the main line. The branch shuttle service, which was usually provided by a small tank engine push-pulling an elderly carriage, stop-ped at a platform on the southern arm of the Ilkeston Junction

triangle. Many trains however continued either to Nottingham or Chesterfield, some using the northern limb which was
devoid of a platform (page 174).

Though Town station possessed but a single platform it was
provided with quite handsome buildings, one facing the main
road and another alongside the platform itself which was
sheltered by a canopy. Unfortunately these admirable facilities were under-used for the branch never did present much
of a challenge to the GNR. Passenger services ceased in 1947
and a bus garage now occupies the site of the terminus. But at
Ilkeston Junction the branch platform can still be detected
and careful observation reveals the former trackbed striking
away through its dismal surroundings.

Another unsuccessful attempt to regain some local traffic
from the GNR was made in 1882 when certain passenger trains
from Ilkeston to Nottingham began to run along the newly-
opened line between Bennerley Junction and Basford. At
least six trains in each direction used the route daily during
the early years of this century, but they were withdrawn as a
World War I economy measure and never reinstated. It is
hardly surprising that the Midland lost interest in its unremunerative passenger facilities at Kimberley for the GNR
offered a far more frequent and convenient service.

The line had opened as far as Watnall Colliery in 1877 and
within two years its double track was carrying through freight
trains. Physically as well as economically it was dominated by
the GNR, for its eastern end lay within sight of Bulwell viaduct, it passed under Awsworth viaduct by an embankment,
and Bennerley Junction stood just below Ilkeston viaduct. A
substantial cutting as well as a short tunnel were required
between Kimberley and Watnall but otherwise the engineering works were light. Some of the line's rails were sent abroad
during World War I, but even this patriotic gesture was
doomed to failure for the ship was torpedoed and its cargo
lost (rails from the Medbourne curve in east Leicestershire
were also aboard). After 1917 the line became a humble
branch from Basford to Kimberley where beer, coal and

general freight were handled.

Though the route has been almost entirely abandoned some interesting relics survive, notably the passenger station at Kimberley (497449). This has been converted into a social club but retains its Midland characteristics including ribbed chimneys and some floral decoration in the brickwork. The adventurous explorer might care to investigate Watnall tunnel which remains intact but can only be reached by negotiating the derelict RAF station, built on one platform of Watnall station, and penetrating the jungle of vegetation which obscures its eastern portal. Another oddity is the isolated brick overbridge standing alongside the M1 motorway north of Nuthall. The little 0–4–4 tanks with their trains of clerestory-roofed coaches seem a far-off cry here!

The Midland made one last effort to consolidate its network in South Derbyshire by building a railway from Butterley to Langley Mill via Ripley and Heanor. Colliery traffic was once again the primary consideration though several mining towns enjoyed an improvement in passenger communications, notably Ripley which had had to be content with the branch from Little Eaton for over thirty years. The section as far south as Heanor was finished in 1890 but trains were unable to connect with the Erewash Valley line before 1895. At Langley Mill the junction faced south, but a short spur turned northwards to end in a bay platform adjacent to the existing station. Its sole purpose was for local passenger trains and a connection with the main line was considered unnecessary. The new railway shunned the old route at Ripley and carved a deep cutting through the town. Consequently, a new station was provided near the market place and the former terminus was reduced to a goods depot known as the 'Old Yard'.

Before World War I, passenger services ran between Nottingham Midland and Ambergate or Chesterfield serving each pit village along the new line. Certain trains took a particularly circuitous route, firstly to Ilkeston Town via Kimberley, then to Ripley by way of Langley Mill, and finally through to Chesterfield Midland. The economic stresses of wartime meant a curtailment of services between Butterley and Langley Mill in the same year as those through Kimberley, but in this case they were started again during 1920. They remained in a feeble state of health however, and despite the introduction of a Sentinel steam railcar in 1925 to cut costs, the deathblow came with the General Strike.

It is still possible to stand on the branch platform at Langley Mill and the two surviving station buildings are well worth examining. That at Crosshill and Codnor, which is used by an engineering firm as a storeroom, is a brick structure incorporating some interesting timberwork (419489). Though the large platform buildings actually in Ripley cutting have been demolished, a compact booking office in smooth red brick still exists at street level (page 173). Particularly interesting is the 'MR' insignia incorporated in one of the gable ends. Regular services were withdrawn from here in 1930 when the Little Eaton line closed to passengers, but holiday specials and miners' excursions which were so characteristic of all the coalfield lines continued for over a quarter of a century (402405).

The Derbyshire Extension Lines

The major factor which shook the Midland out of its complacency was the intrusion of the GNR Derbyshire extension lines into the coalfield area. Having swept round the northern part of Nottingham between Colwick and Basford, the new railway headed towards Eggington Junction where it joined North Staffordshire Railway metals. The line was ready throughout in 1878, but its construction had been a difficult task, for rather than following natural routeways its tracks were laid against the grain of the land and encountered hilly country broken into blocks by broad valleys.

Trains were carried high above the River Leen by a nine-arch brick viaduct at Bulwell, but less than two miles further west they were running through a tremendous limestone cutting punctuated by a short tunnel at Watnall. The Erewash

Valley presented another formidable problem to those responsible for building the railway, but the way in which this was tackled gave the line its most distinctive engineering feature and one which figured prominently in the landscape. Ilkeston viaduct was a steel trestle structure of sixteen spans, each of which consisted of lattice girderwork supported on piers of twelve circular columns braced together and set on stone bases. Its lightweight construction resisted subsidence well, but meant that a speed restriction had to be imposed on trains crossing it. West of Ilkeston the ground undulated less, but cuttings and severe gradients abounded, another viaduct was necessary at Breadsall, and tunnels were bored near West Hallam and Mickleover.

Though an enormous amount of capital was committed to the new railway it proved to be money well spent, for the company captured a large slice of local colliery traffic by way of feeder branches projected along the Erewash and Leen Valleys. Passenger trains worked from Stafford, Burton on Trent or Derby to Nottingham and Grantham, and excursions destined for both east and west coast holiday resorts were very much in evidence during summer months. Regular services west of Derby were withdrawn as early as 1939, but a fairly generous timetable remained in operation over the rest of the line until 1964 when trains ceased to run between Derby Friargate and Nottingham Victoria.

Derby possessed by far the most extensive passenger and goods facilities on the extension lines and they stood nearer to the town centre than the busier Midland premises. In contrast with the wide tract of land bought by the GNR for its western approach to Derby, the lines entered from the east on a narrow viaduct. Friargate itself was a tree-lined street containing dignified Georgian houses and clearly something more elegant than a plain arch or plate girder was required where the railway crossed this fashionable thoroughfare. The resulting bridge was a pleasure to the eye, for its abutments were of stone and its twin spans displayed some richly decorative ironwork incorporating stags derived from the Derby

Urban Nottingham: **Plate 17** (above) *a train of iron ore empties rumbles through London Road High Level station on 30 March 1965;* **Plate 18** (below) *69822 draws a local train out of Carrington station after making an unscheduled stop to set down permanent-way men*

Suburban Nottingham: **Plate 19** (above) *an evening rush-hour train from Victoria to Derby Friargate coasts into Basford North station;* **Plate 20** (below) *67363 leaves Ashwell's tunnel during a tour of the Nottingham Suburban Railway on 6 June 1951*

coat-of-arms (346363).

Far less beautiful was the adjacent passenger station which was an uninspiring affair built on a series of arches. There were four platforms, one at each side and an island between them, but the large timber buildings with their gabled canopies had few architectural merits. Even the booking office left a lot to be desired; it was approached along a short driveway from Friargate but consisted of little more than a wooden shed trapped between the viaduct and a ramp up to rail level. Access to the platforms was by way of a subway and a series of broad staircases, each of which was walled in vitrified buff bricks. Considerably more impressive was the nearby goods warehouse for this was an enormous building and displayed bold ornamental work in red brick.

Other stations between Gedling and Eggington Junction were constructed to a standard design incorporating a single-storey amenities block with a tall station house attached. The roofs were steeply pitched and finished in slate, red bricks relieved with blue brick courses forming the walls. A small timber waiting room was provided on the opposite platform.

Basford North station, though structurally similar to the rest, was built of white limestone embellished with a darker stone giving a peculiar chequerboard effect in places. Once, this was a particularly busy place and formed the terminus of an intensive suburban service from Nottingham Victoria via the 'Back Line' (page 138). Ilkeston North, which was also well used, boasted three platform faces and gained a larger booking office adjoining the roadway some years after the main buildings were opened (page 155).

Most of these buildings have found useful employment as private dwellings or industrial premises, but the impressive GNR viaducts which are so vulnerable to mining subsidence will undoubtedly have to be demolished before long, and the landscape will be so much the poorer without them.

Several branch lines diverged from the main Derbyshire extension and of these the one which ran for $7\frac{3}{4}$ miles along the eastern side of the Erewash Valley between Awsworth and

Pinxton was probably the most important. It opened for coal traffic as early as 1875 and was very much a part of the intensively-mined district through which it passed. The line made an impressive start at Awsworth Junction for it was immediately confronted with the Giltbrook valley which it crossed on a sinuous viaduct of considerable length. This spectacular structure was known locally as the 'forty bridges', though in fact it comprised a wide arch straddling the stream itself, a bridge over the Ilkeston to Kimberley Road and two skew spans across ground-level railways besides the thirty-nine ordinary arches, two of which were blocked to form store-buildings.

With the completion of this viaduct the branch was more or less ready for traffic and the GNR had achieved its main ambition of reaching the rich Erewash Valley coalfield. Nevertheless the company went to the expense of providing five passenger stations, each of which seemed to match its unsavoury surroundings admirably. Eastwood and Langley Mill station was situated where the GNR passed under the main road linking these two places and its platforms were approached by way of staircases leading down from the street-level booking office, an austere structure which stood above the tracks on a girder deck (456471). The fierce red brick of which the whole station was built became blackened with grime as time passed and the place assumed a most inhospitable appearance.

Jacksdale station, which was one of the busiest on the branch, stood in a narrow and particularly industrialised part of the Erewash Valley some three miles north of Eastwood (444516). At this point the railway runs on a viaduct and the platforms as well as the buildings on them were originally of lightweight timber construction. In contrast the booking hall was a damp, dark and depressing room situated beneath the tracks, yet it had an intriguing polychrome brick frontage incorporating arched windows reminiscent of a gothic chapel. Imposing buildings similar to those on the main line were provided at Newthorpe and Pinxton stations. The latter formed the branch terminus and stood on a remote site amid acres of derelict ground which demonstrated just how ruinous the uncontrolled dumping of industrial waste could be (453543).

A passenger service between Nottingham and Pinxton commenced in 1876 and survived until 1963, despite the presence of alternative facilities along the parallel, though less direct, Midland route. In the years preceding their withdrawal the Pinxton branch trains usually comprised an old 0–6–0 tender engine hauling maroon or brown painted suburban stock, though a demoted main line coach occasionally provided an incongruous touch of luxury (page 155). The majority of passengers were workpeople bound for Nottingham or one of the local collieries, but the platforms saw their largest crowds when summer excursion trains wound their way from one Erewash Valley station to the next, picking up holidaymakers destined for such resorts as Scarborough and Skegness. But this railway through the heart of D. H. Lawrence country has ceased to exist and the endless activity on the formerly competitive Midland line only emphasises its delapidation. Even the great Awsworth viaduct, from which passengers enjoyed splendid views of Ilkeston, Heanor, Eastwood and Kimberley, is likely to disappear, though local authorities have urged its preservation as a tribute to the industrial development of the Erewash Valley.

The Leen Valley line was opened in 1882 from the Derbyshire extension west of Daybrook to sidings near Newstead some seven miles further north and represented another major attempt to secure colliery traffic. It kept to the eastern side of the valley as far as Bestwood, veered across the river towards Hucknall, and finally ran through featureless country to its terminus close to a sandstone ridge known as Robin Hood's Hills. Once again, the district had previously been penetrated by Midland tracks and for some considerable distance the two lines lay less than a quarter of a mile apart. In places they ran side by side, near Hucknall they intertwined, and every mine in the vicinity enjoyed the attentions of both companies. But whereas the Midland as firstcomer had been able to choose relatively easy ground, the GNR was forced to adopt a severely graded and sharply curved course. Even then, subsidence played havoc with the formation and over a period of years transformed gentle inclines into severe ones.

Though the stretch north of Hucknall was quite rural, the greater part of the line was dominated by mining in much the same way as the Pinxton branch. Until the early 1930s most Colwick-bound coal trains were hauled by GNR 0–8–2 tank locomotives whose lumbering progress could be heard for miles around. These ungainly machines, which started life on the GNR Northern Heights suburban services out of London, showered the neighbouring fields with red hot cinders and sent a tremendous pall of smoke towards the clouds after the fashion of a volcanic eruption. They consumed such quantities of fuel and water that special coal stages had to be set up at strategic points and a halt at nearly every water column along the way frequently proved necessary. Passenger trains ran initially between Newstead and Nottingham London Road, but once the line had been extended further north most of them continued to Shirebrook and occasionally Chesterfield after Grouping. Victoria station became the southern terminus in 1900 and to reach it Leen Valley services had a choice of routes through Gedling, Sherwood or Bulwell Common.

Though the district was quite adequately served by five Midland stations, the GNR decided to provide a further six along its own branch. Of these, Linby had the most pleasant setting, for the tiny farming settlement near which it stood retained a rustic atmosphere despite the close proximity of a large colliery (533509). The station was made of brick and its main building stood on a deck over the tracks. Hucknall station (page 144) was one of the busiest on the Leen Valley line and structurally had much in common with Linby, though its platforms were marooned between colliery sidings and goods tracks (538492). Butler's Hill station provided a suburb of Hucknall with a train service (543485), but the platforms at Bulwell Forest saw little use, for a golf course prevented the town from spreading towards them (551454).

The limited business provided by the string of small towns along the Leen Valley hardly justified such a density of passenger facilities so Linby was denied its regular GNR train service as early as 1916 and the entire Shirebrook service was withdrawn in 1931, by which time buses had managed to tempt most travellers away from the railway. Coal traffic remained important for another thirty years, but now every length of track has been lifted and the route stands as a thread of wasteland. The site of Leen Valley Junction is occupied by houses and not one of the actual stations remains intact, though railway buildings survive at Linby, Bestwood and Bulwell. A couple of badly-weathered overbridges remain at Hucknall, but certainly the most interesting relic is an ornamental stone and iron structure which the GNR was required to provide across the driveway to Newstead Abbey (524527).

The third GNR branch in the area to acquire a passenger service was the one which ran for $3\frac{1}{2}$ miles along the Nutbrook valley between Ilkeston and Heanor. Though the line passed close to both Coppice and Nutbrook collieries and was indeed built principally to gain yet more coal traffic, it travelled through relatively remote and unspoilt country. The old Nutbrook canal and a private mineral railway kept it company for much of the way to Heanor. A GNR 0–6–0 engine and one carriage often sufficed for the branch service, though the few through workings to Nottingham and the seasonal holiday trains were somewhat more substantial. Heanor station, which was approached by a stairway from the road (425461), consisted of an island platform bearing blocks of well-designed brick buildings (page 144); a similar arrangement existed at Marlpool, the only intermediate station, though access in this instance was from an ornate iron footbridge (443449). The attractive structures as Marlpool were at one time painted according to the wishes of the Mundy family who occupied Shipley Hall, for some of the land required to make the Heanor branch was purchased from them.

As advertised services were withdrawn from the line as early

Heanor GNR and Hucknall Town stations
(from photographs by J. R. Bonser)

as 1928, Heanor gained the doubtful distinction of being the first town in the East Midlands to lose its passenger trains, the alternative Midland facilities having been closed down two years earlier. Neither station was particularly convenient for the town centre and a revival of the GNR branch service in 1939 lasted only two months. Colliery and freight traffic continued for some years, but now that these have gone the line is a wilderness in places and considerable imagination is needed to visualise people boarding trains at Marlpool.

Leen Valley Again

The GNR Leen Valley line remained a branch for eleven years, then in 1893 the MS & L opened its extension from Beighton to an end-on junction with the established tracks at Annesley. Within a very short time work began on the line to London and by 1899 this remote spot near Robin Hood's Hills had become a very busy railway centre. Yet another set of metals was added to the overcrowded Leen Valley and certain towns acquired their third passenger station. At Linby the new line swept across the adjacent tracks of its competitors, continued in a broad arc around the western side of Hucknall, and descended towards Bulwell where it spanned the River Leen by a magnificent blue-brick viaduct of 26 arches. This confident course was reminiscent of the parallel Midland route, but whereas the earlier line had adhered to the valley floor and required few embankments or cuttings, the GCR, whose tracks ran clear of the collieries, was forced to spend a large amount on earthworks.

As the London extension promised to bring a substantial increase in traffic and would demand an enlarged stud of locomotives, the GCR decided to lay out new marshalling yards and build a large motive power depot as the GNR had done at Colwick twenty years earlier. There was sufficient cheap land at Annesley and a six-road shed was built between the GNR and GCR tracks near Newstead Lane (525529). One disadvantage of this location was that the underlying limestone yielded hard water and to make it suitable for engines a softening plant had to be installed. There was also a grim timber lodging house for crews whose duties had brought them far from home. This gained a reputation for its abundance of rats, and only a colony of colossal cats kept their numbers down to a reasonable level. Freight locomotives predominated at Annesley. Various 0-6-0 tender and 0-6-2 tank types were used for colliery traffic while large 2-8-0 engines hauled long-distance coal and goods trains, especially those along the London extension to Woodford.

When Arkwright Street shed was virtually abandoned because of high water rates in 1909, Annesley inherited several 4-4-0 and 4-4-2 express engines as well as 4-4-2 tanks for local trains, but after Grouping, Colwick took over responsibility for the majority of such passenger duties and the Leen Valley depot returned to housing mineral engines for the most part. During the 1960s, however, several ex-LMS and LNER 4-6-0s for general traffic, a number of 2-10-0 engines for heavy freight work, and a few main line locomotives such as 'Royal Scot' 4-6-0s and 'Britannia' Pacifics for coping with the remaining Marylebone expresses were to be seen at Annesley.

Many men based at the depot lived in Nottingham, Bulwell or Hucknall and to get them to or from this isolated place a special train composed of decrepit carriages drawn by a pensioned-off locomotive ran between the shed yard and Bulwell Common station, usually along the main line but sometimes via the less-congested GNR route after Grouping. It was known as the Dido and for several years some vintage Sacré 2-2-2 and 2-4-0 engines spent a leisurely retirement doing this duty. At first the rolling stock consisted of four-wheel carriages with wooden seats, but less spartan clerestory-roofed vehicles eventually replaced them and a Clayton steam railcar was tried in the 1930s, but this proved unsuccessful.

Inside the Dido the air reeked of twist tobacco smoke and the floor was usually covered with onion peelings, cigarette ends and dead matches. When the carriages did get their infrequent sweep-out it was either in Bulwell station, to the despair of the station master, or at Annesley where a little embankment of rubbish accumulated alongside the Dido siding. Once, an innocent young fireman tossed an empty packet on a compartment floor already ankle-deep in debris. On seeing this a weatherbeaten old driver poked the lad with his pipe and informed him in a droll voice that they didn't allow that sort of thing and everybody was responsible for keeping the place clean! Whether the youngster ever retrieved his discarded litter will never be known, but at some later date he no doubt played a similar trick on some unsuspecting novice. As Annesley declined the characters disappeared and so did the Dido. The celebrated train was ignominiously replaced by a Trent bus; the motor vehicle had triumphed even here (page 156).

Hucknall Central and Bulwell Common were the two conventional stations on this section of the GCR, the former having the larger accommodation. Both were built with island platforms and displayed the Jacobean style of architecture so typical of the London extension. Halts were erected at Hollinwell & Annesley and Bulwell Hall for the convenience of the golfing fraternity, while an even more primitive structure for the benefit of shed staff and drivers existed in the open spaces near Newstead Lane (527529). Annesley South consisted of a rough sleeper platform and a timber shed which was swept out even less than the Dido. Its ancient burnt-out stove provided little comfort on a bleak day, but certain local passenger trains as well as the Dido stopped here, and they were the means of getting home.

The Leen Valley still echoes the rumble of coal trains, but these run only on the former Midland line which has itself been reduced to a mere colliery branch between Radford and Annesley. Both tunnels which pierced Robin Hood's Hills have now been abandoned and filled with colliery spoil. As far as passenger facilities are concerned it is reasonable to argue that the over-capitalisation of the last century has been replaced by the opposite state of affairs, for once there were sixteen stations in the six miles between Bulwell and Annesley; now there are none.

CHAPTER 8

Between Mansfield and Chesterfield

The Beginnings

During the latter part of the nineteenth century an intricate
network of railways spread over north-east Derbyshire and
north-west Nottinghamshire. Once again, exploitation of the
abundant and high quality coal reserves was the major factor
in their development. The growth of this part of the coalfield
came much later than such areas as the Erewash Valley, so
canals and their associated waggonways were confined to the
periphery. As late as 1870 the few colliery branches that did
exist were based on the Midland line between Chesterfield
and Pye Bridge. A cover of barren rocks which rendered the
seams less accessible was partly responsible for this delayed
progress but with improvements in technology deep mines
were sunk further east and now feature prominently in the
Dukeries and Sherwood Forest landscapes. So, despite a sluggish start, the railway system between Mansfield and Chesterfield grew rapidly from 1870 to 1900 and still plays a vital
part in the transportation of coal. The expansion of passenger
services was similarly brisk, but their importance was destined
to be short-lived.

Mansfield Midland station was once the focus of an intricate
web of lines and boasted more daily passenger trains than St
Pancras. Seventy years ago these local services were the life-

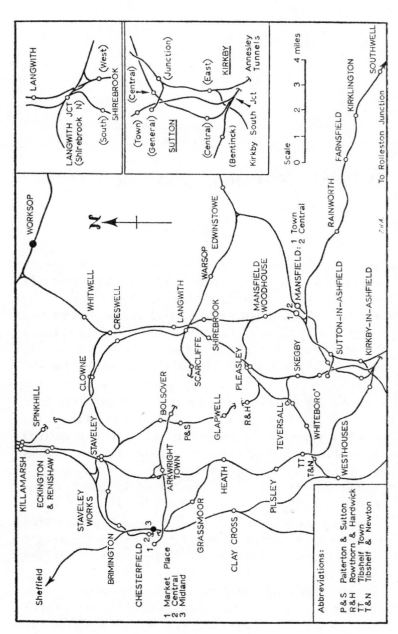

Map of the railways between Mansfield and Chesterfield

blood of the coalfield, but gradually they felt the effects of road competition and one by one fell victims to policies of rationalisation. When the last train left Mansfield for Nottingham Midland during October 1964, the town became the largest regional centre in England without a passenger station.

The first rails to Mansfield were those laid in 1819 from the canal wharf at Pinxton. It was a horse-operated line intended for general goods traffic, though from 1832 a passenger carriage operated on market days. With construction of the Erewash and Leen Valley lines, the Mansfield & Pinxton Railway, having been acquired by the Midland, was rebuilt to main-line standards in 1848. But it was not until 1875 that the company began to establish itself north of Mansfield by extending the line to Worksop.

Another link which proved valuable for coal traffic had opened between Mansfield and Southwell in 1871. The latter place, a small but ancient town with a magnificent Norman cathedral, had been served by a short branch from the Nottingham to Lincoln line since 1847. This little railway had experienced rather uncertain beginnings, including a period of horse traction when there was but one train a week. But the opening of the Mansfield line saw a through service from Southwell to Buxton, reputedly because of the influence of the bishop whose diocese included the Derbyshire town. This soon came to an end, and afterwards, a couple of trains a day provided the local service to Mansfield.

Unfortunately, the 12½-mile journey between the two towns regularly took up to 40 minutes, and though farmers bound for market never demanded a cracking pace, this was too bad. The line gained such a reputation for docility that, rumour has it, it was possible to alight at Rainworth, walk to the local hostelry, and consume two unhurried pints before rejoining the same train. During 1929 the service finally expired leaving Southwell on a branch from Rolleston Junction once again. This push-pull service lasted until 1959 and was provided by an old Johnson 0-4-4 tank engine with one carriage.

Specials for Southwell racecourse, which adjoins Rolleston

Junction station, and excursions for east coast resorts continued to work from coalfield towns through Mansfield and Southwell until the line closed (page 173). Coal, however, was of far greater importance. Blidworth (1926) and Bilsthorpe (1928) collieries brought new life to the western end of the line and caused the LMS to double the Southwell to Rolleston Junction track as well as build a new west to south curve to the Nottingham line. Now that much of the track has been lifted, and the remote red brick stations at Farnsfield and Kirklington have been converted into dwellings, the very lonely wolds surrounding the upper Greet Valley seem far from the industrial sprawl. Only distant chimneys betray the collieries which once made the line busy.

Coal Fever

Travelling through north Derbyshire today, it is impossible to realise how indispensable the long-forgotten passenger trains which once connected Mansfield, Alfreton, Pleasley and Staveley were to the little communities which they served. They ran on minor railways which were built initially as outlets for the newly sunk collieries. When buses proved a more convenient link with civilisation for the miners and their families, the tracks continued to serve the purpose for which they were built.

In 1863 a branch from Westhouses was opened as far as Teversal and extended along the Meden Valley as the coalfield developed eastwards. Eventually the Pleasley to Woodhouse link was completed enabling a through passenger service between Mansfield and Alfreton to begin in 1886. This was vital to the small townships which had mushroomed alongside the pits, for their overnight growth had left them far from self-sufficient, and for other than immediate needs they looked to Mansfield. From the 1890s to the General Strike the smart little Midland trains were well used.

Kirtley or Johnson 0-4-4 tank engines which were equally happy running with chimney or bunker first normally provided motive power for the four non-corridor carriages. Mansfield depot provided both locomotive and crew for the 37-minute journey to Alfreton, and though this was again an undistinguished schedule for 12½ miles, the crimson lake engine and carriages made a delightful sight on the winding single track with its mixed backcloth of cornfields, wooded valleys and collieries. Though most of its passengers were making local journeys, the service connected with St Pancras expresses at Alfreton and provided a convenient route from Mansfield to London. But this was insufficient to make the trains profitable, and the LMS withdrew regular services in 1930.

From Westhouses to Pleasley Colliery the rails remain in daily use, but the section along picturesque Pleasley Vale, where the River Meden flows through a limestone gorge, has been abandoned. The railway ran high above the river and passengers were treated to pleasant views of the steep wooded banks with the Hollins Cotton Mills below. Little survives of the once busy stations, but in the Railway Inn at White-borough old miners still like to recall the time when their station was the best kept in England (460601).

Further north lies the Doe Lea Valley which experienced 'coal fever' in 1872 when a massive exploitation of local seams began with the establishment of Ireland, Bolsover, Bonds Main and Glapwell collieries. By then the Midland feared for its security in view of threatened advances by alien lines and, as the new pits were sunk, hastily extended its metals south-wards to claim the traffic. Eventually the line reached Pleasley enabling a Mansfield and Chesterfield service to begin in 1890. In a direct line these places are only just over eleven miles apart, but the twisting rail journey stretched the distance to 20 miles and took 55 minutes. It was frequently necessary to change trains at Staveley, so the through traveller needed both patience and resilience. The Doe Lea Valley trains also ceased in 1930.

In their heyday, these little railways which wandered past drab pit heaps and sidings were considerably enlivened by the privately owned coal wagons displaying a variety of colours with large letters advertising their ownership: BOLSOVER, SHIREBROOK, SHERWOOD. Other characteristic sights were the trains of ancient carriages nicknamed 'Paddy's Mails' which took pitmen to their work. It was common for men who could ill-afford the weekly shilling ticket to attempt a free ride, and when railway officials and police came aboard the fare dodgers would be seen scattering across the fields.

South of Glapwell the line grew tired of the mining valley and climbed through a tunnel piercing the Bolsover ridge to reach open agricultural land west of Pleasley. Soon after passenger trains ceased, the rails through the subsiding tunnel were removed. It then found employment as a mushroom farm and during the war was used for storing ammunition, but now it is blocked. Beyond it the wooded grounds of Hardwick Hall were visible, and a station providing for the nobility there ensconsed, as well as the hamlet of Rowthorne, was built. Though this building has long since been reduced to rubble, two precious reminders of busier days survive at Bolsover and Glapwell. The latter place has lost its permanent way, but the friendly little station building in dark red brick now serves as a meeting place for the Full Revival Gospel Mission. A similar structure remains in railway employment at Bolsover Castle (page 156).

Penny Emma

Sutton in Ashfield saw the last new length of Midland line in the area. In an attempt to strengthen its position at that town before competition arrived, the company opened a short branch from the main Mansfield line at what purported to be Sutton station to a modest terminus near the town centre. Soon after it opened in 1893, the branch was burrowed under by two rival companies which provided their own stations in Sutton, so what traffic the Midland had cultivated was rapidly eroded. The shuttle service did provide a useful connection with trains to Attenborough for the townspeople who worked

Derbyshire extension: Plate 21 (above) *Ilkeston North station showing the extra platform provided for the Heanor service;* Plate 22 (below) *69453 eases a Pinxton branch passenger train into Pye Hill & Somercotes station*

Railwaymen only: Plate 23 (above) the Annesley 'Dido' enjoying more than generous motive power near Bulwell Common on 14 September 1959; Plate 24 (below) a train of empties bound for Glapwell Colliery pauses at Bolsover Castle station to pick up permanent-way men

at Chilwell Ordnance Depot, but in times of economic stress it was vulnerable and suffered temporary withdrawal during World War I and the General Strike. The workmen's service finally ceased in 1951, though many of the older inhabitants of Sutton still recall as youngsters having a jaunt 'down t' junction on ol' Penny Emma' in the 1930s (page 174).

An Invasion

By 1890 the Midland's monopoly of the north Nottingham-shire and Derbyshire coalfield was coming to an end. The next twenty-five years saw a massive influx of competitive lines, no less than 80 miles of them having been opened by 1900. Ambitious local concerns established themselves at Chesterfield and Mansfield, while both the Manchester, Sheffield & Lincolnshire Railway and the Great Northern expanded into territory which Derby regarded as its own. The MS & L came first, having obtained an Act for a line from Beighton to Annesley in 1889. The railway passed through Staveley, climbed to over 550ft and swept down to Kirkby in Ashfield before entering a deep cutting. This led to a 1,000yd tunnel which pierced Robin Hood's Hills and gave access to the Leen Valley where a junction was made with the existing GNR line.

Though intended as a first step towards the much wanted independent route to London, the new line crossed rich coal reserves, and over ten miles of colliery branches built with the main line exploited this traffic. Ironically, the subsidence caused by mining prevented really fast running when London expresses used the route, though the bold earthworks and confident curves across the hills were clearly intended for speed. Elegant dining-car expresses of varnished teak carriages hauled by magnificent green locomotives became an everyday sight in the Derbyshire landscape. A less distinguished local service benefited mining communities such as Heath, Pilsley and Tibshelf, while the endless procession of freight trains carrying steel from Sheffield, fish from Grimsby and coal from

South Yorkshire made this railway a true artery of the nation.

Coal traffic certainly yielded a handsome revenue, but mining disfigured the once pleasant countryside with mountainous heaps of shale, some a menacing black, others burnt raw red. First-class passengers might have felt mild discomfort as their Marylebone express passed Heath, and the acrid smell from Holmewood coke ovens penetrated the dining-car. They might have noticed the station master at Heath turn from his lunch and wave his knife and fork to the crew of the *South Yorkshireman* as it pounded past his track-side house on the climb up Staveley bank. Perhaps they caught a glimpse of the old wooden station buildings, the Industrial Co-operative shop or the Miner's Welfare next to an austere pub. It was another world beyond the carriage window.

Now the trains have gone. Lifeless hollows and weed-infested banks mark the course of shining steel rails, and where millions travelled in comfort only a Pennine breeze disturbs the grass. One by one the expresses, stopping trains and freights were withdrawn or diverted, and the former main line was reduced to a colliery siding. As the pits closed the rails retreated, and near Tibshelf the M1 motorway irreverently severs the trackbed, a reminder that a new artery has emerged. Derbyshire County Council is making an admirable attempt to reclaim derelict land and remove the industrial scars from these attractive hills. Now their usefulness has ended, the great cuttings are being filled with colliery waste bulldozed from ugly tips. Substantial progress has been made north of Annesley tunnel, at Tibshelf, and at Pilsley where cattle graze on renewed land that has been given a Countryside Award. Those Great Central expresses might never have passed this way.

Despite such destruction, the old MS & L station building at Kirkby Bentinck continued to stand on a curve in the track above the Erewash headwaters (488555). Around lay the ruins of colliery sidings overlooked by the old houses whose inhabitants once depended on the railway. With its gabled canopies and ornate ironwork the wooden structure still retained a

Victorian atmosphere, though several years of neglect were shown by the peeling veneer of maroon and cream paint. But in 1972 this last reminder of the MS & L Derbyshire lines was irreverently smashed to pieces.

A Grim Loop Line

Besides the Beighton to Annesley line, the 1889 Act sanctioned a branch from Staveley to Chesterfield which not only afforded the MS & L access to this important market town but also served Staveley ironworks (423750). Well before the spur was completed, the Sheffield directors saw considerable advantages in continuing it beyond Chesterfield to rejoin the main line at Heath, thus creating a loop. But, whereas the original branch pursued a comparatively easy route along the Rother Valley, the extension involved a hefty climb out of Chesterfield and required a tunnel under the town itself.

The loop was far from scenic, especially the lengths near Sheepbridge and Staveley Works where a clinging smog frequently hung in the damp Rother air during winter months. From a train, derelict land seemed abundant, especially near the stagnant Chesterfield Canal. The ceaseless clatter of machinery and clanking of wagons still dominates the old blackened cottages of Whittington Moor, though railway activity is now confined to former Midland metals and the abandoned loop lies forlorn. Amid this desolation, the little wooden building which once served as Brimington station (392737) has managed to survive both the polluted air and bleak winds from the moors, as well as twenty years of redundancy.

At Chesterfield, the MS & L did little to improve the town's amenities when forced to tunnel through a shoulder of land flanking the River Rother. Excavations took place below a built-up area and the approach cuttings were dismal places walled in blue bricks. One would have thought that a comparatively short tunnel of considerable bore with houses above would be without a smoke vent, but the MS & L provided an extra large one which broke the surface behind an old house in Spa Lane (386710). The garden of this unhappy dwelling is entirely occupied by a vast pit. Through the iron grid, which is surrounded by a low wall, residents were afforded an unenviable prospect of the trains below. If this vulgar intrusion was insufficient reminder of the railway, then the generous doses of soot and sulphur from locomotives blasting southwards certainly were. Here the tunnel profile flattened to accommodate the foundations of houses only a few feet above. Everyone hereabouts knew when Great Central trains were passing: no wonder the famous spire twisted a little more each year!

Chesterfield Central station closed on withdrawal of the loop passenger service in March 1963, since when its timber buildings have been destroyed and all available space used to store cases of sweet jars from an adjoining factory. The station was on a slight curve and had two spacious platforms with a carriage storage siding between the main through lines. A bay was provided for Sheffield local trains at the bleak north end where ornate canopies gave little protection from the draughts. But the really gloomy outlook was at the town end. Access to both platforms was provided by covered staircases leading down from the large booking office carried on a steel deck across the tracks (page 176). Beneath it, lines converged on the dreary cutting and into the smoky tunnel mouth beyond, while behind the awnings and finials rose a silhouette of houses crowned by that grotesque spire.

The train that rumbled out of the dusk and ground to a halt had probably called at all stations from Nottingham or Leicester. Its opening carriage doors revealed not businessmen or smart commuters but miners, steelworkers and railwaymen themselves. Neither brief case nor umbrella were to be seen. Flat caps, old coats, greasy overalls and snap tins proliferated, for this railway was as much a part of industrial north Derbyshire as the blast furnaces, belching chimneys and winding gear. Now hardly anything remains of this once familiar scene, and the Victoriana that was Central has gone.

An Ambitious Pauper

Chesterfield once boasted a third station in addition to the defunct Central and the surviving Midland where express trains still call. Many people would find it hard to believe that a dignified three-storey building which stands near the market square was once a railway terminus. For the frontage which directly adjoins the pavement and has a long glass canopy is reminiscent of a theatre, while beyond the buffer stops a spread of new buildings and car parks occupy former railway property.

But this was Chesterfield Market Place, the headquarters of a local line with the grand title of Lancashire, Derbyshire & East Coast Railway. A scheme was conceived by William Arkwright, a local landowner, for an independent outlet for coal mined on his estate east of Chesterfield. In 1891 a Bill was obtained for a massive railway from Warrington, on the Manchester Ship Canal, to Sutton on Sea, a village on the Lincolnshire coast where it was intended to build docks suitable for exporting coal. Inevitably this adventurous coast to coast scheme ran into financial disaster, and only the central section between Chesterfield and Lincoln was ever constructed. From its opening in 1897 to absorption by the Great Central in 1907, the East to West, as the line was known, built up a considerable traffic in coal worked largely by its own locomotives. But passenger business was never great, despite attempts to encourage tourists to visit the aristocratic properties north of Warsop by designating the line 'The Dukeries Route'.

Inside Chesterfield station was a glass-roofed concourse from which led four curving platforms. At one of them simmered an ageing tank engine prepared to pull its three non-corridor coaches over the coalfield hills and across the Trent plains to Lincoln (page 175). It was an interesting journey over the now abandoned section to Langwith Junction, for the line was a succession of ascents and descents acrosss the grain of the country and demanded two splendid viaducts as well as a tunnel nearly a mile and a half long. Unfortunately, mining subsidence played havoc with these structures and the railway suffered a premature death brought about by the very pits it was built to serve.

Before leaving Chesterfield the line crossed an impressive viaduct consisting of brick arches, lattice deck girders and a large bowstring span, together carrying the LD & EC over both Midland and Great Central metals besides the polluted River Rother (387705). In this landmark, from which passengers obtained a grand panorama of the old town rising away to the north, the LD & EC saw a ready-made hoarding for its slogan 'The Dukeries Route' which was applied in large letters. Now the viaduct has been dismantled, except for a few brick pillars where, it seems, the demolition gang grew tired.

Unlike the terminus which was treated in Jacobean style, local stations were devoid of decoration and looked very much alike with their low red brick buildings featuring flattened arches recessed into the wall and shallow roofs with squat chimneys. It is necessary to visit Ollerton to see a well-preserved specimen, for those in the industrial areas west of Langwith have been destroyed. Arkwright Town was the gloomiest. Its name recalls the man who started the railway and everywhere around it are collieries and the little hamlets with peculiar names such as Cock Alley, Furnace Hillock and Winsick that owe their existence to coal.

Another great viaduct spanned the Doe Lea Valley where Midland metals were already established, but ahead loomed the limestone escarpment dominated by Bolsover Castle. This formidable barrier was conquered by a 2,624yd tunnel through which double track climbed at 1 in 120. Even in the driest weather it was raining inside Bolsover tunnel, for water seeped continuously through the porous rock, and after fifty years the great work was crumbling from dampness besides sinking through subsidence. It had become so dangerous by 1951 that the passenger service to Chesterfield was abandoned, the track through it lifted, and its portals and shafts sealed. At its eastern end the ascent continued in a spectacular rock chasm to Scarcliffe station and it is necessary to step perilously close to the edge for a glimpse of the tunnel mouth deep below.

By far the busiest LD & EC station was Langwith Junction, renamed Shirebrook North in 1924. The main building, which was a longer version of the standard design, contained a refreshment room in its heyday. At one time, trains departed for Chesterfield, Lincoln, Sheffield and Nottingham, but when the last summer holiday trains ran in 1964 its four platforms became redundant and only the rumble of coal wagons echoed round this grim place.

Langwith Junction was so named because it marked the start of a branch to Beighton where connections were made with the Midland and, from 1907, Great Central metals. At the summit of this line was Clowne, a classic north Derbyshire industrial town where old pubs serve best Mansfield or Worksop ales and resound with talk of collieries and horse racing. Clowne had two stations. The first was opened by the Midland Railway in 1888 on a single-track branch. Separated from it by a driveway was the LD & EC establishment, a far larger affair opened in 1897 with two platforms approached from a street level booking office on a brick arch under which the rails passed. A curious feature was a waiting room attached to the side of the goods shed.

Clowne was originally the branch terminus, but from 1900 the service was extended to Sheffield, in which form it continued until withdrawn in 1939. This did not mean the end of passenger workings over this route, however, for in connection with the Great Northern Leen Valley Extension (see below) it provided a useful alternative when the main Great Central line between Beighton and Kirby South Junction was closed for track repairs or by a derailment. On one occasion the newly out-shopped Pacific *Flying Scotsman* hauled the diverted 'Master Cutler' this way. On another, a B1 4–6–0 shook the cuttings along the 1 in 100 climb through Killamarsh and Spinkhill as it struggled unassisted with fourteen coaches. But such diversions are now neither necessary nor possible, for track has been removed from most of the route and the short sections that do remain are dependent on the fortunes of individual collieries for their future existence. The 'Clog and Knocker', to give the LD & EC its locomen's nickname, has served its purpose.

More Great Northern

Kirkby South Junction lay in a remote rock cutting west of Annesley tunnel which carried MS & L tracks through Robin Hood's Hills (500552). From this point sprang two railways which linked the main line with former LD & EC metals and provided alternative outlets for colliery traffic previously carried by the Midland.

The first was built by the Great Northern Railway which, having found its earlier adventures into the Nottinghamshire and Derbyshire coalfield highly remunerative, sought to spread its tentacles even further. But the Bill deposited in 1891 for an extension of the Annesley branch northwards to Shirebrook had retaliatory overtones too, for King's Cross saw its interests threatened if the vigorous attempts being made by the MS & L to obtain a main line to London came to fruition. When Parliament dismissed this scheme, a somewhat relieved GNR directorate withdrew plans for its own line. However, having promptly thought better of this decision, powers for the Leen Valley Extension were acquired in the following session.

The promise of lucrative coal traffic must have been strong, for this new GNR enterprise was a costly affair. Not only were some of the rock excavations massive, but everywhere the impression given was of a very solidly built railway. Blocks of the tough yellow limestone blasted from deep cuttings were employed in bridge abutments and station buildings. A tunnel north of Annesley was avoided by exercising running powers over the MS & L to Kirkby South Junction and, in spite of undulating terrain, not a single viaduct was required. But earthworks were impressive along the route northwards from the Erewash headwaters, through Sutton in Ashfield and down the Meden Valley. Most dramatic of all was the descent into Langwith. Leaving the River Meden at Pleasley Vale, the line entered a sheer rock cutting over a mile long (518663). Beyond this lay Shirebrook station and almost immediately the falling ground demanded a sweeping embankment on which the rails were carried high above the town.

The grandest passenger accommodation on the line was at Sutton in Ashfield where the GNR facilities were not only the most centrally situated, but also the most impressive of four stations which once served the town. A street level booking office overlooked the track from a massive girder deck which also carried the roadway. Covered stairways led to each platform where smaller buildings contained waiting accommodation, toilets and porters' rooms. Regular blocks of rough-hewn limestone gave the buildings a harsh though durable external appearance, but inside the rooms a proliferation of glazed tiles and intricate dark woodwork displayed an opulence characteristic of the GNR at this time. Unfortunately, passenger traffic hardly did justice to such expensive architecture and the station stood derelict for several years: a grand monument to unfulfilled hopes.

About a mile further north lay a smaller though no less interesting station built to serve the township of Skegby. Here, communication between the booking office and high-level platforms was achieved by covered stairways connected by a subway. In what remains more or less a rural setting, such urban characteristics appear oddly out of place. Over forty years have elapsed since regular passenger trains to Nottingham Victoria rumbled to a stand overhead and the glazed cream bricks echoed the latecomer's hurried footsteps, but even today it is not impossible to imagine the scene in these dim passages (page 175).

Teversal is an attractive farming village which has somehow managed to escape the desecrating effect of industrial housing, despite being overshadowed by the massive Silverhill and Teversal collieries. The GNR constructed a branch railway from Skegby to tap these pits, and so enthusiastic was the company for its share of coal traffic that this line opened almost five years before the through Shirebrook service was able to start. But Teversal itself had a passenger station. It was built with a proper platform, brick waiting rooms and offices, and a fine station house, all of which remain. Perhaps there were plans to run a regular public service, but in fact only miners' 'Paddy' trains and seaside excursions ever ran. At one time the colliers had their own places in the ancient carriages. Besides keeping their compartment reasonably tidy they provided candles themselves, for the vehicles had no lights, and anything they did not wish to take down the pit was left on their seat, where nobody ever interfered with it.

While the LD & EC Railway maintained an independent existence, GNR trains terminated at their own station in Shirebrook. Even when extended to Langwith Junction, they duplicated existing services in the larger towns and at intermediate places served a comparatively sparse population which eventually turned to the buses. So during 1931 passenger facilities were withdrawn from the former GNR line. However, when local trains ceased to run on the Mansfield Railway (see below), Sutton in Ashfield was left with only the remote Junction station and, as an experiment, British Railways re-opened the old GNR establishment in 1956. With gushing optimism, council dignitaries rode with the first departure to Nottingham and the front of Sutton station received a lick of maroon and cream paint. But local people complained of badly timed trains, especially the evening one which left Victoria at 10.25pm, before cinema and theatre shows had finished. Almost inevitably, the venture died through lack of support after only eight months.

Along with the Langwith Junction to Beighton line, this GNR branch provided the necessary relief for the congested GCR main line, as already noted. Fast freight trains regularly came this way and from 1962 to 1964 a sleeping car train from Glasgow to Marylebone disturbed the silent stations during the small hours. But it was coal that gave birth to the line and coal that supported it. When the line was youthful, a string of colourful colliery wagons hauled by a GNR 'Long Tom' 0–8–0 was a familiar sight. Fifty years later, dull trains of standard steel hoppers trundled along behind soot-coated Austerity 2–8–0s. But the load was the same. When coal traffic was diverted to formerly competitive Midland routes, the Leen Valley Extension became redundant. Gaunt limestone cuttings which had long echoed the struggles of powerful locomotives on full regulator became desolate, lonely places. At Shirebrook, where trails of smoke once drifted endlessly over the old terraced streets, only a pathetic skyline of broken bridges and crumbling banks remains.

The Mansfield Railway

Kirkby South Junction was also the beginning of the Mansfield Railway, one of the last standard gauge lines of any length to be built in the East Midlands, and certainly the last to offer a regular public passenger service. Its stations came into use as late as 1917, almost a year after stopping trains on the Nottingham Suburban Railway had ceased. That the passenger and freight services had a brief existence is hardly surprising in an area already congested with permanent way.

As with so many Nottinghamshire railways, initiative for the Mansfield line was concerned with coal rather than the promise of a lucrative passenger business. As mining spread eastwards into Sherwood Forest, vast new collieries, many with their attendant townships, began to transform the legendary preserves of Robin Hood into a thriving industrial area. Mansfield Colliery (570614), started by the Bolsover Company in 1905, had a potential output of over one million tons a year and its owners were not happy about the prevailing Midland monopoly which, as far as Mansfield was concerned, neither the GNR nor GCR seemed enthusiastic to challenge. So when a proposed LD & EC branch foundered, local enterprise launched the Mansfield Railway Company under the chairmanship of J. Plowright-Hufton, managing director of Bolsover Collieries. In 1910 Parliament authorised nearly eleven miles of railway from Kirkby South Junction to the former LD & EC line at Clipstone. When it emerged that the newcomer would convey some three million tons of coal annually from Clipstone, Rufford and Mansfield Colleries, the larger companies began to show interest, and it was the Great Central which agreed to operate and maintain the line for 60 per cent of its gross earnings. Much of the coal was to be taken by the GCR to Immingham Docks for export.

That colliery traffic would pay handsomely was never in doubt, but the optimistic predictions for passenger services proved unrealistic, especially at Mansfield which, it was hoped, would benefit from a new main line. Although through carriages ran to Marylebone and a Leeds to Bournemouth express came this way between the wars, most long distance traffic consisted of summer Saturday holiday and excursion trains destined for east coast resorts from Scarborough to Skegness. Ordinary trains provided an all-stations service from Edwinstowe to Nottingham Victoria, but as many workings ventured no further north than Mansfield, they merely supplemented parallel GNR and Midland facilities.

The largest and most frequently used station was the gaunt affair at Mansfield Central (543609). From a train it appeared bleak and drab with platforms of coarse planking partly sheltered by awnings (page 176). A railed-off stairway descended into the gloom. But the track crossed eastern Mansfield by a succession of embankments and girder bridges so that the same buildings which seemed undistinguished from the platform rose to an impressive four storeys externally (page 169). Long and lofty though its facade was, the structure lacked width and appeared peculiarly wall-like. The harsh, red brick walls were sparingly relieved by a cornice and parapet in stone, and especially by a small tower which recalled best Great Central Jacobean and served to house the parcels lift. The gable ends were treated rather pleasantly with broken pediments, but a truly delightful detail was the inclusion of

Mansfield Central station, exterior

stained glass in the large second floor windows intended as part of a refreshment room which never materialised. A modest canopy extended along the frontage, at one end of which was a grand stone entrance providing access to the tall and very sombre blue brick booking hall. This had a ticket window to the left, a stairway for the Nottingham platform on the right, and a white-tiled subway to Edwinstowe trains straight ahead.

Most passengers were southwards bound from Mansfield, so a bay platform was provided for Nottingham trains. Here, before grouping, a GCR 4–4–2 or 0–6–2 tank engine from Annesley shed was commonly seen at the head of a passenger train. Later, when Colwick shared the work, ex-GNR loco-motives appeared, including 0–6–0 tender and 0–6–2 tank classes. In later years, before the last train on 31 December 1955, it was even possible to see a powerful GCR 4–6–2 tank, which had spent more hectic days working crowded suburban trains out of Marylebone, prepared to lead its three non-corridor coaches down to Kirkby South Junction and along the Leen Valley towards Nottingham Victoria.

The route south of Mansfield exhibited several features of interest, certain of which may still be observed for the time being. As the rails left the town for open country they curved over the dam of a picturesque mill reservoir known locally as the duckpond and here the formation is more or less complete (532597). Sutton in Ashfield Central station survives and has been kept in good condition. It is a neat little red brick building with a cumbersome platform canopy but graceful porch (504586). Here the line entered a cutting in which it stayed past the erstwhile Summit Colliery to Kirkby in Ashfield station now demolished, but friable sands and clays encountered during excavations necessitated strong masonry retaining walls up to nine feet thick. Beyond Kirkby the line dropped steadily across the head of the Erewash Valley to Kirkby South Junction where further large-scale excavations, this time in hard limestone, were necessary to lead the rail-way to the main line.

After little more than half a century of use the Mansfield Railway was dismantled. North of the town a branch from Clipstone is retained for access to the collieries which dispatch coal via the sprawling concentration sidings (606642), but modern diesel locomotives handle the traffic. The GCR 0–6–0s and 2–8–0s which trundled above the Mansfield with heavy freight trains have disappeared, as has so much of the line itself. Already there are places where its course has been almost totally eradicated (550613); the enterprise and determination shown by colliery owners and townspeople alike in the first decade of this century might never have existed. The Mansfield Railway, as with so many once-busy lines in the East Midlands, has been forgotten.

Gazetteer

The following notes have a twofold purpose. Firstly, they aim to provide essential background information including the opening dates, changes of ownership and closure sequence for each of the railways mentioned in the text; secondly, they attempt to establish a record of the more interesting physical remains, the most important historical sites and the outstandingly scenic sections of every line so described.

Only those relics whose continued existence seems reasonably assured have been entered. Buildings, structures and earthworks which merit inclusion but are likely to have disappeared by the time this register appears in print have been excluded. Nevertheless, seemingly permanent features may suddenly be destroyed whereas certain derelict buildings can be rescued and renovated. Though this has been taken into account as far as possible, discrepancies are quite likely to occur.

Probably the best way of gaining an initial impression of the East Midland railway system is to take a series of journeys by train along the surviving routes. Such excursions also present an opportunity to pause at the towns and cities where worthwhile remains of abandoned lines may be visited on foot. The following itineraries are suggested:

(a) *Northern area; access from Sheffield:*

Midland backwaters: **Plate 25** (above) *84008 at Ripley with a special train on 21 April 1956;* **Plate 26** (below) *a Hucknall to Rolleston Junction race excursion passes Blidworth & Rainworth station on 28 March 1959*

Midland termini: **Plate 27** (above) *a well-coaled LMS 2–6–4 tank waits at Ilkeston Town with a Nottingham train on 27 June 1933;* **Plate 28** (below) *the 'Penny Emma' ready to leave Sutton in Ashfield for Mansfield*

Across the hills: **Plate 29** (above) *the 4.00pm train for Lincoln stands at Chesterfield Market Place station on 19 July 1948;* **Plate 30** (below) *42897 leads a Pleasley East to Dudley excursion out of Skegby on 2 August 1959*

Central stations: Plate 31 (above) *horse-drawn carriages waiting outside Chesterfield Central when it still bore traces of its MS&L ancestry;* Plate 32 (below) *a local train for Nottingham Victoria standing at Mansfield Central station during the 1930s*

Sheffield–Chesterfield–Derby–Matlock–Derby–
Nottingham–Sheffield
(b)   *Southern area; access from Nuneaton:*
      Nuneaton–Leicester–Stamford–Leicester–Nottingham–
      Grantham–Nottingham–Leicester–Nuneaton.

Ironically, the only efficient way of examining a number of
the more remote sites in one visit is by using a car, and there
is ample material in each of the eight regions to take up a
whole day. For those with sufficient energy, certain particularly attractive stretches of track are worth examining on foot
and the possibilities are listed in the gazetteer. The precise
location of all sites is given by an appropriate six-figure grid
reference for the relevant Ordnance Survey map. The One-
Inch sheets covering the area are as follows: 103, 111, 112,
120, 121, 122, 123, 132, 133, 134. Although there is some
overlap in figures at the extreme edges of the area it should
be immediately obvious to which district each refers.

   Abbreviations have been used as follows:

ACT: Date of Act of Parliament.
OPD: Opening dates of lines and services.
CSD: Closure dates of lines and services.
REMS: Remaining features of interest.
SETTING: Interesting landscape features adjacent to line.
USES: Present employment of former railway build-
              ings and trackbed.
Pass: Passenger traffic.
Gds: Goods traffic.

An asterisk after certain items indicates that the locality is
particularly worth visiting.

HIGH LEICESTERSHIRE

BELVOIR CASTLE RAILWAY   1½ miles
Horse railway, 4ft 4in gauge; owned by Duke of Rutland.
OPD: 1815   CSD: 1918
REMS: Muston Gorse Wharf by Grantham Canal (818359);
rails in grounds of Belvoir Castle (819338).

SAXONDALE AND BOTTESFORD–
WELHAM AND DRAYTON   45 miles

Great Northern and London & North Western Joint Railway.
ACTS: Newark–Melton Mowbray (GNR): 6 August 1872;
Melton Mowbray–Leicester (GNR): 28 July 1873; All GNR
& LNWR Joint lines and vesting of Bottesford–Marefield section into joint ownership: 30 July 1874.

OPD: Saxondale Junction–Melton Mowbray: July 1879
(Gds); 1 September 1879 (Pass); Bottesford–Stathern: 15
December 1879 (Gds & Pass); Melton Mowbray–Welham
Junction: 15 December 1879 (Gds & Pass); Hallaton–Drayton Junction (Medbourne branch): 15 December 1879 (Gds);
2 July 1883 (Pass).

CSD: Bottesford South station: 1 May 1882; Bottesford south
to west curve: 1882; Passenger service over Medbourne
branch: 1 April 1916; Bingham Road station: 2 July 1951;
Redmile station: 10 September 1951; All local passenger services: 7 December 1953; Unadvertised workmen's trains
Leicester–John O'Gaunt: 29 April 1957 and Market Harborough–East Norton: 20 May 1957; Summer excursion
trains Leicester–Mablethorpe & Skegness via Melton Mowbray & Bottesford: 9 September 1962; Saxondale–Barnstone
closed entirely, and Bottesford south to west curve reinstated:
1962; Goods south of Marefield: 4 November 1963; Melton–
Colwick goods: 7 September 1964; Barnstone cement sidings:
1968; Bottesford–Redmile still used for very occasional oil
deliveries.

REMS: *Bottesford:* South station site (798389); *Redmile:*
station houses, more ornate than average to match now-demolished station (787362); *Harby & Stathern:* houses, bridge,
lengthy driveway (762315); *Long Clawson & Hose:* north
portal of 834yd tunnel (746265); *Scalford:* south portal of
tunnel, deep cutting, combined aqueduct and road bridge
(746254)*; *Melton Mowbray:* Sysonby curve—used to bring
construction materials via Midland and removed 1882
(743186); *Thorpe Trussels:* substantial cutting, overbridge
(729128)*; *Twyford:* John O'Gaunt viaduct (741092)*; *East*

Norton: viaduct (790009)*; station house, cottages, north portal of 444yd tunnel (793003)*; *Hallaton*: prospect of station from village, station houses (794966)*; *Medbourne*: station house, remains of platforms (801934).

SETTING: The section of line which climbed up from the Vale of Belvoir, pierced the escarpment by Hose tunnel, and emerged in typical Leicestershire Wold country is best seen by taking the Harby–Hose–Scalford road. A length of line which passed through characteristic High Leicestershire landscape was that between John O' Gaunt and East Norton: follow the Twyford–Marefield–Whatborough–Tilton–Loddington–East Norton roads to appreciate it. From above East Norton tunnel the descent towards the Welland valley is admirably seen.

USES: At Great Dalby and Hallaton the trackbed has reverted to agricultural use.

LEICESTER BELGRAVE ROAD–MAREFIELD 10¼ miles
Great Northern Railway.
ACT: 28 July 1873.
OPD: Goods: May 1882; First Skegness excursion: 2 October 1882; passenger services: 1 January 1883.
CSD: Marefield west to south curve (on withdrawal of Leicester–Peterborough service): 1 April 1916; local passenger services: 7 December 1953; Unadvertised workmen's service Leicester–John O' Gaunt: 29 April 1957; Excursions to Mablethorpe & Skegness: 9 September 1962; Through goods trains: 1 June 1964, after which access to Belgrave Road was by reinstated Forest Road spur (used during construction of line and removed 1882); Belgrave Road goods: 14 December 1964; Humberstone coal yard: 1 May 1967; Catherine Street petrol depot: 1 January 1969.
REMS: *Leicester*: Belgrave Road goods depot (592057); *Humberstone*: station house, cottages (612054); *Ingarsby*: smoke vent and portals of 516yd tunnel (669050)*; viaduct (682055); station building, house, cottages (687057)*; *Lowesby*: station house, cottages (736070).
USES: Belgrave Road station site forms part of an urban

motorway. The trackbed through built-up Leicester has largely been taken up by housing and industrial developments. Ingarsby station has been converted into an attractive dwelling.

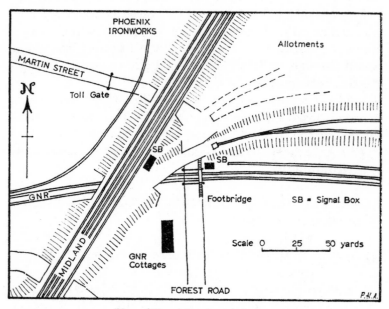

Plan of Forest Road area, Leicester

IRONSTONE RAILWAYS

Owned variously by GNR, Midland and private companies; numerous isolated bridges and earthworks survive around Eastwell.

REMS: *Waltham*: old station used by GNR race trains; closed as goods depot in 1964 (799268); *Eastwell*: incline down to exchange sidings on joint line (764287); *Holwell*: substantial cutting, stone overbridge (734246).

WEST OF LEICESTER

SWANNINGTON COMMON RAILWAYS   2 miles
Horse railways; owned by Leicester Navigation.

OPD: 1794   CSD: 1798
REMS: *Thringstone*: cuttings (419181 and 421179); *Pegg's Green*: embankment (415177); *Swannington Common*: embankment (418172)*.

TICKNALL TRAMWAYS   18 miles
Horse tramways, 4ft 2in gauge; owned by Ashby de la Zouch canal.
OPD: 1802–36   Absorbed by Midland Railway: 1846
CSD: 1850–1916
REMS: *Ticknall*: bridge over main street (356240)*; 138yd tunnel (355236)*; 50yd tunnel (352232)*—both tunnels may be reached by footpaths from the village; embankment (3492 27); stone blocks (348224)*; *South Wood*: bridge (358209); *Willesley*: embankment (343154).

SWANNINGTON–LOUNT   2¼ miles
Swannington & Worthington Rough Railway (horse-operated).
OPD: 1833
CSD: 1872; Lount–Newbold relaid as colliery line in 1925; closed again: 1968.
REMS: *Newbold*: 90yd tunnel (399189)*; *Pegg's Green*: rails in situ across road (409178)*; embankment and remains of underbridge (406181).

LEICESTER WEST BRIDGE–SWANNINGTON 16 miles
Leicester & Swannington Railway.
ACT: 29 May 1830.
OPD: West Bridge–Bagworth (Stanton Road): 17 July 1832 (Pass & Gds); Bagworth–Ashby Road (Bardon Hill); 1 February 1833 (Gds); 22 February 1833 (Pass); Ashby Road–Long Lane (Coalville): 22 April 1833 (Gds); 27 April 1833 (Pass); Long Lane–Swannington: 25 November 1833 (Gds only); Soar Lane Branch: 4 October 1834 (Gds only).
Absorbed by Midland Railway: 1 January 1847; new route between Knighton Junction and Coalville, including Thornton deviation: 27 March 1848 (Gds); Passenger services

extended to Burton on Trent: 2 October 1848, diverted to Leicester (Campbell Street): 1 August 1849.

CSD: West Bridge–Desford passenger service: 24 September 1928; Swannington spur and incline: 14 November 1947; West Bridge goods yard: 4 April 1966. The Leicester to Coalville line is still in use for goods traffic (closed to passengers: 7 September 1964).

REMS: *Glenfield*: west portal of 1,796yd tunnel (545065)*; east portal of tunnel (562062); smoke vents at intervals through housing estate*; *Thornton*: Stag & Castle Inn—site of supposed accident on 4 May 1833 (458081)*; *Bagworth*: incline and contractor's cottage—reached by lane from main road near colliery (446091)*; *Swannington*: incline, stone bridge over stream (418164)*. Also—stone blocks in wall at former Bardon Hill station (443126); Soar Lane lift bridge at Leicester Museum of Technology; Swannington engine in York Museum; section of track in Kensington Science Museum.

SETTING: It is well worthwhile investigating the full length of both Bagworth and Swannington inclines, though sturdy footwear is essential.

USES: Glenfield tunnel has been put at the disposal of the Civil Defence for emergency use; West Bridge yards are being redeveloped for industry; much of the remaining trackbed through Leicester is disappearing under housing schemes.

PEARTREE & NORMANTON–ASHBY DE LA ZOUCH
Midland Railway.   15 miles

ACT: Breedon–Ashby (conversion from Ticknall tramway): 5 July 1865.

OPD: Derby–Ashby passenger service: 1 January 1874.

CSD: Local passenger services: 22 September 1930.

Smisby Road (Ashby)–Melbourne occupied by War Dept from 19 November 1939 to 31 December 1944 as Melbourne Military Railway. Burton Road to Lount closed soon afterwards and Lount to Worthington closed during 1968.

REMS: *Ashby de la Zouch*: traces of branch platform (3541 63); course through town; crossing house (355168)*; *Old*

Parks: northern portal of 447yd tunnel, cutting, exchange wharf with tramway—can only be reached by taking lengthy footpaths from Smisby or Lount roads (364187); *Worthington*: traces of station (408210); *Breedon*: station building (416240)*; *Chellaston*: station building and house (376300)*. USES: Breedon station is now a house; Chellaston station is a workshop.

OVERSEAL & COALVILLE–NUNEATON & HINCKLEY

London & North Western and Midland   27 miles
(Ashby & Nuneaton) Joint Railway.
ACTS: 17 June 1867; 25 June 1868 (modifications to route).
OPD: August 1873 (Gds); 1 September 1873 (Pass)—except Hinckley branch.
CSD: Overseal station: 1 July 1890 (on extension of LNWR services to Burton and Ashby); local passenger services: 13 April 1931; most goods facilities: 1964; Market Bosworth goods yard: 1968. The railway between Overseal and Measham is still used for colliery access.
REMS: *Measham*: station buildings (332119); *Shackerstone*: station buildings and house (379066)*; *Market Bosworth*: station buildings and house (393031); *Stoke Golding*: station buildings—note different style (392973)*; *Ambion*: two brick bridges typical of those on the line (399987).
SETTING: Overbridges and trackbed of Hinckley branch as well as the adjacent Ashby Canal are worth exploring near Higham on the Hill. The scenery around Shackerstone is the most pleasant on the line.
USES: Individual stations—Measham: motor showroom; Market Bosworth: garage; Stoke Golding: scrapyard; Shackerstone: occupied by Midland Railway Society who plan to reopen the line southwards to Shenton.

COALVILLE–LOUGHBOROUGH   10½ miles
Charnwood Forest Railway.
ACT: 16 July 1874   OPD: 14 April 1883
Worked by LNWR from outset; adjudged bankrupt: Novem-

ber 1885; resumed its own management: 1 July 1909.

Thringstone, Grace Dieu, Snell's Nook halts opened: 1 April 1907.

Absorbed by LMS: 1 January 1923.

CSD: Local passenger services: 13 April 1931; excursion traffic: 1951; Loughborough goods yard: 31 October 1955; remaining goods services: 7 October 1963; Shepshed quarry traffic: 12 December 1963.

REMS: *Loughborough*: goods shed (528201); three-track locomotive shed—along lane off Derby Road (527200)*; *Shepshed*: station buildings (477186)*; *Tickhill Lane*: typical brick bridge (463186); original Charnwood Forest Canal aqueduct used to carry railway—may be reached by footpath from main road (459185)* (below); *Whitwick*: station buildings and forecourt (435162)*.

SETTING: The best impressions of the railway may be obtained at Tickhill Lane, Grace Dieu and Whitwick; note the changing panorama of Charnwood itself.

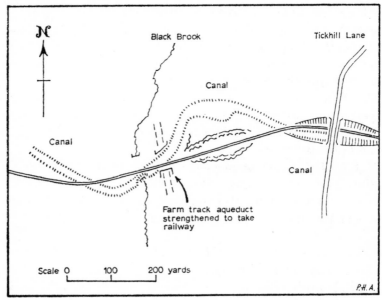

Plan of Charnwood Forest Railway near Blackbrook

USE: Individual buildings—Shepshed station: private house; Whitwick station: ironmonger's shop; Loughborough engine shed: garage; Loughborough, Shepshed and Whitwick goods sheds: warehouses.

SWADLINCOTE LOOP LINE 7¾ miles
Midland Railway.

Swadlincote branch—ACT: 3 August 1846; OPD: 1 July 1851; Woodville branch—ACT: 16 July 1846; OPD: 1 April 1859; Swadlincote to Woodville (new station)—ACT: 29 June 1875; OPD: 12 April 1880 (Gds); 1 May 1883 (Pass); Woodville (new station) to Woodville Goods Junction on the original branch—ACT: 17 June 1878; OPD: 1 September 1884 (Gds & Pass).

CSD: Local passenger services: 6 October 1947; Blackpool excursion trains: 8 September 1962; goods traffic: 1964, western section still in use to serve Cadley Colliery.

REMS: *Woodville*: station buildings of original terminus which closed in 1883 (315194)*; northern portal of 307yd tunnel—can be reached from site of new Woodville station (319189); *Swadlincote*: goods yard buildings and former platform in use as a retaining wall (299199).

SETTING: The intensely industrialised nature of the route can be best ascertained from an overbridge south of Woodville (316184).

USES: Woodville old station is in use as a storeyard; much of the loop trackbed has been annexed by industrial concerns.

BURTON & ASHBY LIGHT RAILWAY 11½ miles
Midland Railway; 3ft 6in gauge electric tramway.

ACT: 5 November 1902. OPD: 13 June 1906 CSD: 19 February 1927.

REMS: *Ashby de la Zouch*: rails in forecourt of station (355163)*; *Swadlincote*: bridge built to carry tracks over loop line, car sheds (300199)*; *Newhall*: reserved section between Sunnyside and High Street (288210)*; posts which supported overhead wire in High Street (290208) and Sunnyside (2862 11)*.

SETTING: Much of the tramway ran along ordinary town streets and country roads, but the reserved section between Bretby and Newhall made a clear path across the fields and is worth tracing (285218).
USES: Part of the reserved track near Sunnyside is a timber yard; car sheds at Swadlincote are NCB Central workshops.

GROBY QUARRY RAILWAY   2 miles
OPD: 1832   CSD: 1966
REMS: *Groby*: Granite-faced south portal of tunnel (5220 73); granite bridge under main street (523077).

CLIFFE HILL QUARRY RAILWAY $2\frac{1}{4}$ miles
OPD: 1897; 2ft 0in gauge.   CSD: 1948
REMS: *Billa Barrow*: Rails in cutting and across lane in two places (465113); embankment constructed in 1911 (468111).

BETWEEN SYSTON AND PETERBOROUGH

LORD HARBOROUGH'S CURVE $1\frac{1}{2}$ miles
Midland Railway.
ACTS: 30 June 1845 (for Syston & Peterborough Line); 18 June 1846 and 22 July 1847 (deviations for Lord Harborough's curve).
OPD: Melton–Stamford section of s & p: 20 March 1848 (Gds); 1 May 1848 (Pass); New curve and station at Saxby: ACT: 24 June 1889; OPD: 28 August 1892, when old station and curve were closed.
CSD: Saxby new station and goods depot (latter on western part of old curve); 6 February 1961.
REMS: Old station house (812193)*; crossing cottage (8141 94)*; bridge (824185). A large part of the curve may be covered on foot; much of it has reverted to agricultural use but there is dense vegetation in places. Note remains of Oakham Canal—bought by Midland on 27 July 1846 (page 187).

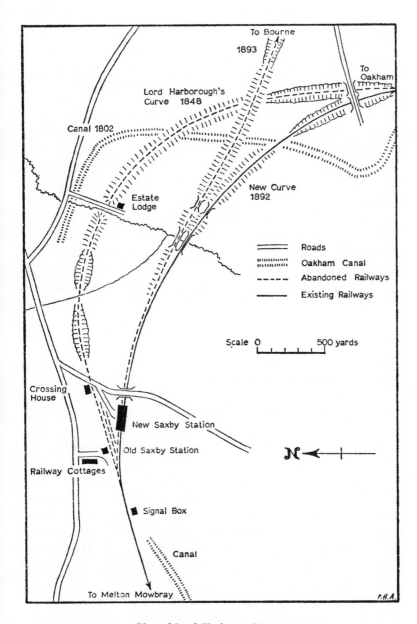

Plan of Lord Harborough's curve

SAXBY–LITTLE BYTHAM 13 miles
Midland Railway.
ACT: 24 June 1889.
OPD: 5 June 1893 (Gds); 1 May 1894 (Pass).
CSD: All passenger services: 2 March 1959; goods services by 6 April 1964. Between Wymondham and South Witham 2 miles of line remain to give access to Market Overton Quarries (closed 1 January 1972, but the site of a preservation scheme).
REMS: *Saxby*: blue brick viaduct (819191); *Wymondham*: station building (852191)*; *South Witham*: station building (925190).
USES: Edmondthorpe & Wymondham and South Witham stations have both been converted into houses; The South Witham to Castle Bytham road assumes the course of the old formation for ¾ mile to alleviate a crossing with a main A1 road (934192); A factory occupies the trackbed at South Witham.

STAMFORD–ESSENDINE 4 miles
Stamford & Essendine Railway.
ACT: 15 August 1853. OPD: 1 November 1856
Worked by Great Northern Railway until 1 January 1865 when S & ER became responsible for operating its own trains; GNR resumed working line: 1 February 1872; Leased to GNR; 15 December 1893.
CSD: Stamford East station: 4 March 1957—trains diverted into Stamford Town; passenger services: 15 June 1959; Stamford East goods yard: 4 March 1963; Priory sidings: 1969.
REMS: *Stamford*: station building, train shed, goods warehouse (034069)*; timber trestle viaduct over R. Welland— reached by footpath from St Leonard's Priory (041074)*; *Essendine*: brick viaduct over R. Glen (051117).
USES: Stamford station has become living accommodation; the train shed and goods yard buildings are used by a haulage firm.

STAMFORD–WANSFORD 8½ miles
Stamford & Essendine Railway.
ACT: 25 July 1864.   OPD: 1 February 1867.
Historical details as above.
CSD: All passenger services: 1 July 1929; freight: by 1931.
REMS: *Barnack*: station buildings, goods office (083053)*; *Wansford Road*: station buildings, house, goods yard buildings (089996)*.
SETTING: Very rural nature of the line can be seen from overbridge near Southorpe (083023).
USES: Barnack station is now offices; Wansford Road station is now a dwelling.

PILTON QUARRY RAILWAY 4 miles
OPD: 1919   CSD: 1969.
REMS: A typical deserted ironstone line of the district: note long, gorge-like quarries, exchange sidings, steep climb from main line, reversing neck to give access to workings (923027).

CENTRAL LEICESTERSHIRE

LEICESTER LONDON ROAD–RUGBY 20¼ miles
Midland Counties Railway.
ACT: 21 June 1836.   OPD: 1 July 1840.
Incorporated into Midland Railway on 10 June 1844.
CSD: All passenger services and goods facilities: 1 January 1962; Newbold Wharf (Rugby): 3 May 1965; Line between Leicester and Wigston North Junction still part of main route to London.
REMS: *South Wigston*: Crow Mills viaduct, embankment (588977)*; *Broughton Astley*: a good example of an original brick bridge (539926), station house, staggered platforms either side of road (535920)*; *Ullesthorpe*: station house (507876); *Rugby*: viaduct across Avon valley (502766)*.
USES: A factory occupies the trackbed at Wigston. At Countesthorpe the route is obscured by a housing estate—but

notice the Railway Inn and its sign serving as a reminder of the line.

RUDDINGTON–RUGBY $38\frac{3}{4}$ miles

Great Central Railway.

ACT: 28 March 1893.

OPD: July 1898 (Coal); 15 March 1899 (Pass).

CSD: Ruddington, Rushcliffe Halt, Quorn & Woodhouse, Rothley, Belgrave & Birstall and Whetstone stations: 4 March 1963. Through Nottingham Victoria–Marylebone trains: 5 September 1966; Nottingham Arkwright Street–Rugby Central passenger service, together with East Leake, Loughborough Central, Leicester Central, Ashby Magna, Lutterworth and Rugby Central stations: 5 May 1969; Line north of East Leake is retained for gypsum traffic—this will eventually be diverted southwards on to Midland route via new connection at Loughborough; An attempt is being made by the Main Line Preservation Group to reopen a section of line between Loughborough and the outskirts of Leicester.

REMS: *Loughborough*: viaduct and embankment across Soar valley (542217)*, Central station (543193)*; *Quorn*: station buildings (549162); *Swithland*: section of line across the reservoir, remains of uncompleted station—archway in underbridge (563132)*; *Rothley*: station buildings (568122); *Birstall*: deep cutting, station buildings (588084)*; *Mowmacre Hill*: massive brick arch over road and embankment above it (586078); *Leicester*: viaduct across city between Harrison Street (582056) and Western Road (580039)—this contains many individual items of especial interest, such as the larger bridges, vault for Roman pavement (582046) and site of Northgate Street collision (582051), and can be closely examined by walking along the adjacent streets*; Central station frontage (582047)*, goods offices in Western Boulevard (581040)*, Upperton Road viaduct across the railway (579034); *Whetstone*: 13 arch viaduct across the Sence valley (558984)*, station-access from road underbridge (555976); *Ashby Magna*: cutting and 92yd Dunton Bassett tunnel (552900)*; *Newton*:

5 arch skew road bridge (530786); *Rugby*: viaduct of 14 brick arches, 3 plate girders and 2 lattice girder spans, the latter over the LNWR main line (516758)*.
SETTING: The section between Rothley and Quorn is especially attractive.

HIGH DERBYSHIRE

PEAK FOREST TRAMWAY   7 miles
Horse tramway, 4ft 2in gauge.
OPD: 1799.   Absorbed by MS & LR: 1863.
CSD: 1924–5.
REMS: Much of the route can be traced, especially near Chapel Milton, Chapel-en-le-Frith and Barmoor Clough— alongside the Buxton branch railway (073797)*

CROMFORD–WHALEY BRIDGE   33 miles
Cromford & High Peak Railway.
ACT: 2 May 1825.   OPD: Cromford Wharf–Hurdlow: 29 May 1830; Hurdlow–Whaley Bridge: 6 July 1831. Connections with other railways—at Cromford: 21 February 1853; at Whaley Bridge: 17 August 1857. Leased by LNWR: 30 June 1862; Absorbed by LNWR: 19 July 1887.
   Realignments—near Hurdlow: 2 January 1869; near Hindlow: 25 June 1892 (in connection with the construction of the Ashbourne to Buxton line).
   Passengers carried between 1855 and 1877.
CSD: Shallcross–Ladmanlow: 25 June 1892; Shallcross–Whaley Bridge: 9 April 1952; Ladmanlow–Old Harpur: 2 August 1954; Middleton Incline: 12 August 1963; Middle Peak–High Peak Junction: 9 April 1967; Middleton Top–Friden Brickworks: 21 April 1967; Friden Brickworks–Parsley Hay: September 1967.
REMS: *Cromford*: workshops and transit shed alongside canal (314559)*; Sheep Pasture incline and catch-pit containing debris of wagon from 1965 accident (311560)*; *Middleton*: engine house, engine and boilers, incline (2755

52)*; *Hopton*: 113yd tunnel (266548)*; incline (253546)*; *Longcliffe*: station house with stable, acute curve in trackbed, old metal bridge over Ashbourne to Rowsley road (225557)*; *Minninglow*: stone-faced embankment (207566); *Gotham*: very acute curve in trackbed (188585); *Newhaven*: 51yd tunnel with carvings over each portal (151629)*; *Hurdlow*: incline (124662); *Burbage*: 580yd tunnel (032739)*; *Bunsall*: incline (022752); *Shallcross*: incline (014800); *Whaley Bridge*: incline and wharf (012814).

SETTING: A walk along the whole section between Cromford and Parsley Hay is well worthwhile for the energetic. Also worth examining is the stretch above Hindlow incline, abandoned in 1869. The route between Bunsall incline and Burbage tunnel is an interesting walk—but stout footwear should be used.

USES: The southern half is destined to become the High Peak Trail. Much of the trackbed between Fernilee and Whaley Bridge has been covered by buildings. Both Bunsall incline and one mile of formation south of Burbage tunnel have become roads.

MATLOCK–BUXTON   19¾ miles
Matlock–Rowsley: *Manchester, Buxton, Matlock & Midland Junction Railway.*
ACT: 16 July 1846.   OPD: 4 June 1849.
Leased jointly by MR and LNWR: 1 July 1852.
Absorbed by MR: 1 July 1871.
Rowsley–Buxton: *Midland Railway.*
ACT: 25 May 1860.   OPD: Rowsley–Hassop: 1 August 1862; Hassop–Buxton: 1 June 1863.
CSD: Individual stations: Rowsley (original terminus): 1 August 1862; Hassop: 17 August 1942; Monsal Dale: 10 August 1959; Great Longstone: 10 September 1962 (one morning train continued to make an unadvertised stop for the benefit of a nurse at Buxton hospital). Local passenger services: 6 March 1967; Manchester to St Pancras expresses diverted: 1 April 1968; Rowsley and Bakewell goods depots:

1 July 1968 (through freight diverted previously). The line from a point west of Miller's Dale is in use to give access to Buxton for freight traffic.

REMS: *Darley Dale*: station buildings (272626)*; *Rowsley*: original MBM & MJR station and nearby cottages (259660)*; new station (258658); *Bakewell*: station buildings (222690); *Hassop*: station buildings (217705); *Great Longstone*: station buildings (197711)*; *Miller's Dale*: viaducts (southern one: 1862; northern one: 1905), station platform and surviving buildings (137733).

SETTING: From Monsal Head Hotel (184715)*: superb panorama of Monsal Dale with viaduct and track formation. Descend along footpath to inspect western portal of 533yd Headstone tunnel and for close view of viaduct. From road near Cressbrook (168731)*; prospect of 515yd Litton tunnel and 471yd Cressbrook tunnel, with trackbed on shelf between them. Whole section between Monsal Head and Miller's Dale is worth investigating and use can be made of the many footpaths along the valley.

USES: Station buildings occupied as follows: Darley Dale: engineering firm; Rowsley old: offices for road construction plant firm; Rowsley new: packing case store; Hassop: agricultural engineering firm; Great Longstone: private house.

BUXTON–ASHBOURNE   22½ miles
London & North Western Railway.
Line incorporated 2¾ miles of C & HPR route.
ACT: 4 August 1890.   OPD: Buxton-Parsley
Hay: 27 June 1892 (Gds); 1 June 1894 (Pass). Remainder: 4 August 1899.

CSD: Hindlow station: 15 August 1949; Local passenger services: 1 November 1954; excursion traffic and emergency winter services as well as most freight facilities: 7 October 1963; Hartington coal yard (served by branch from Buxton): 2 October 1967; Section of line between Hindlow and Buxton is retained for quarry traffic.

REMS: *Ashbourne*: tunnel—both portals, but northern

one most accessible (176469); *Thorpe Cloud*: station house (166504); *Tissington*: station cottages (177522); *Coldeaton*: deep limestone cutting (160575)*; *Hartington*: brick and stone viaduct, station houses, signal box, station driveway cut through limestone (149611)*; *Fenny Bentley*: goods warehouse (173511); *Mapleton*: girder bridge with blue brick abutments typical of lower part of line (174484); *Alsop en le Dale*: stone arch bridge typical of higher part of line where some need to blend with the landscape was felt (154551).

SETTING: A glimpse of Dovedale (152561); view from Parsley Hay station site (147636); a walk along the whole section between Ashbourne and Parsley Hay is well worthwhile, again for the energetic.

USES: Trackbed from Ashbourne (Mapleton Lane) to Hartington has been transformed into the Tissington Trail. Most intermediate station sites serve as car parks. Hartington signal box is employed as a warden's office. A weigh hut at Alsop en le Dale has been converted into a shelter.

CLAY CROSS–ASHOVER   7¼ miles
Ashover Light Railway; 2ft 0in gauge.
ACTS: 4 December 1919, 13 November 1922, 2 August 1924.
OPD: Goods to Fallgate: 1924; Passenger & Goods throughout: 7 April 1925.
CSD: Regular passenger services: 3 October 1931; Summer season passenger services: 13 September 1936; Mineral traffic: 31 March 1950.
REMS: *Fallgate*: station building just inside quarry entrance (355621)*; *Clay Cross*: carriage body and former 'Rainbow' cafe alongside bowling green (399639)*; *Dalebank*: trackbed and flood arches (360616); *Chesterfield Road*: embankment and remains of bridge over main road (390645).
SETTING: Sections at Dalebank and between Fallgate and Ashover Butts give a good impression of the scenery through which the line passed.
USES: Much of the former trackbed has returned to agri-

cultural use. Near Walley (370609) over a mile of the formation has been submerged beneath Ogston Reservoir.

CITY OF NOTTINGHAM

EARLY RAILWAYS   Approx 5 miles
Several horse-operated lines associated with the Nottingham Canal were built in the Strelley area during the early 1800s. More famous is the ancient wooden trackway which was laid from Wollaton Lane to coal pits at Strelley. The Wollaton Railway was almost certainly in operation by 1604 and is thought to have been Britain's earliest surface railway.

NOTTINGHAM–MELTON MOWBRAY $18\frac{1}{4}$ miles
Midland Railway.
ACT: 18 July 1872.
OPD: 1 November 1879 (Gds); 2 February 1880 (Pass); 1 March 1882 (St Pancras expresses).
CSD: Edwalton station: 28 July 1941; Plumtree: 28 February 1949; Goods facilities at Edwalton & Plumtree: 1 November 1965; Through expresses: 18 April 1966 (except one each way daily which was withdrawn on 1 May 1967); Line between Edwalton and Melton is retained for use by the Advanced Projects section of British Rail.
REMS: *Nottingham*: Trent bridge (584387)* *Plumtree*: station building (618324).

COLWICK–NOTTINGHAM LONDON ROAD $2\frac{3}{4}$ miles
Ambergate, Nottingham, Boston & Eastern Junction Railway.
Grantham–Colwick:
ACT: 16 July 1846.   OPD: 15 July 1850.
Colwick–London Road:
ACT: 3 July 1854.   OPD: 3 October 1857.
Worked by GNR from 2 April 1855; Title changed to Nottingham & Grantham Railway & Canal Company: 1860: Leased to GNR: 1 August 1861; Connection with Midland at Colwick removed in 1866 (interchange between two systems afterwards

afforded by link at London Road); Absorbed by LNER; 1 January 1923.

CSD: Passenger trains between Trent Lane Junction and London Road Low Level: 22 May 1944; Connection with Midland at Colwick reinstated: 10 January 1965; Trent Lane –Colwick: 3 July 1967 (Pass); 25 May 1968 (Gds); Trent Lane–London Road Low Level still used for parcels traffic.

REMS: Platform at Racecourse station (596395); section adjoining Colwick Woods, including stone overbridge (601 397).

COLWICK–BASFORD   7 miles
Great Northern Railway.
ACT: 25 July 1872.

OPD: September 1875 (Coal); 1 February 1876 (Pass); Colwick shed & yards: 1878–9.

CSD: 4 April 1960 (temporarily); 12 March 1962 (permanently); Daybrook goods facilities: 1 June 1964; Colwick LNWR shed: 10 September 1928; Colwick GNR shed: 13 April 1970; Colwick–Mapperley still used for colliery traffic.

REMS: *Colwick*: London North Western Terrace (6284 05)*; *Gedling*: station buildings (622423)*; smoke vent of 1132yd Mapperley tunnel (599443).

USES: Gedling station has been converted into a youth centre. Housing development covers the trackbed at Arnold and Daybrook. Mapperley cutting is being filled with colliery spoil.

TRENT LANE–DAYBROOK   3½ miles
Nottingham Suburban Railway.
ACT: 25 June 1886.   OPD: 2 December 1889.
Worked by GNR from outset. Absorbed by LNER on 1 January 1923.

CSD: Intermediate stations: 13 July 1916; Reduced to single track: 9 February 1930; Through passenger trains: 14 September 1931; Pick-up goods service to all stations withdrawn: 1 August 1951.

REMS: *Trent Lane*: remains of flyover and sharp down-line curve at 1 in 49 (590393); *Thorneywood*: north portal of 128yds Sneinton tunnel (592407), station house, footbridge, retaining wall, portal of 118yd inclined tunnel to Nottingham Patent Brick Company's Works (592410)*, south portal of 408yd Thorneywood tunnel (591413)*; *St Ann's Well*: station house (589420)*, cutting (586425)*; *Sherwood*: north portal of 442yd Sherwood tunnel, traces of platforms, over-bridge carrying Mapperley Rise, bridge and incline of Mapperley Brickworks line (581430)*, 70yd Ashwell's tunnel—may be walked through (580434)*; *Daybrook*: underbridge at Thackeray's Lane (582442)*.

USES: Alongside Colwick Road a public house occupies the site of embankment near where bomb dropped on 8 May 1941. An electrical firm's storeyard occupies trackbed at Sneinton Boulevard. Thorneywood station site is now a GPO depot. St Ann's Well station site is occupied by a housing development. Sherwood station now bears two tower blocks of flats.

TRENT LANE–WEEKDAY CROSS   1 mile
Great Northern Railway.
ACT: 28 March 1893.
OPD: 24 May 1900 (though certain through GNR trains used the line from 15 March 1899).
CSD: London Road High Level station and all passenger trains: 3 July 1967. The line is temporarily retained in connection with Ruddington gypsum trains.
REMS: Viaduct which forms greater part of line; High Level station frontage (579394)*.
USES: High Level station is an office furniture storeroom.

BULWELL COMMON–RUDDINGTON   7¾ miles
Great Central Railway.
ACT: 28 March 1893.
OPD: July 1898 (Coal); 15 March 1899 (Pass); Nottingham

Victoria Station: 24 May 1900 (jointly built by GCR and GNR). CSD: Carrington station: 24 September 1928; Manchester–Marylebone trains: 3 January 1960; Local Nottingham–Sheffield services together with Bulwell Common, Arkwright Street and Ruddington stations: 4 March 1963; New Basford station: 7 September 1964; through passenger trains north of Nottingham (Bournemouth–York) and semi-fast service to Marylebone: 5 September 1966; Nottingham Victoria station: 4 September 1967 (on which date Arkwright Street was re-opened); Goods facilities at New Basford and Queen's Walk (near Arkwright Street): October–November 1967; Mineral trains between Bagthorpe Junction and Weekday Cross Junction: 25 May 1968; Arkwright Street station and Rugby passenger service: 5 May 1969; Weekday Cross–Ruddington section is temporarily retained in connection with gypsum trains.

REMS: *Carrington*: station buildings at roadside, sandstone cutting, south portal of 662yd Sherwood Rise tunnel, north portal of 1,189yd Mansfield Road tunnel (568416)*; *Central Nottingham*: Victoria station clock tower, cutting and retaining walls adjacent to south portal of Mansfield Road tunnel (574403)*, Thurland Street—built over cut and cover tunnel, Cross Keys Inn (rebuilt) where navvies entered beer cellar, Weekday Cross Junction, cutting, south portal of 392yd Victoria Street tunnel (574396)*; *The Meadows*: viaduct—especially the span across Midland station—and Arkwright Street station buildings (574389)*, Trent bridge (571381).

USES: Victoria station site has been redeveloped as a huge complex of shops, flats and entertainments known as the Victoria Centre. Carrington station buildings (street level) have become a shop and poodle parlour. Arkwright Street station buildings (street level) have become car-hire offices—high level part demolished January–March 1973. Bagthorpe Junction area is being cleared for industry. The whole of the Meadows and the GCR line along with it will eventually be replaced by modern housing. Victoria Street tunnel is to be retained to carry large pipes in connection with area central heating scheme, whatever the fate of the headshunt.

NORTH AND WEST OF NOTTINGHAM

EARLY RAILWAYS   Approx 50 miles
In the late eighteenth and early nineteenth centuries some forty horse-operated railways (excluding the Little Eaton Gangroad and Mansfield & Pinxton Railway) were built to carry coal from local pits to the Cromford, Erewash, Nutbrook and Nottingham Canals. The vast majority of these were to be found along the slopes of the Erewash valley between Pinxton and Stapleford.

LITTLE EATON GANGROAD   9¼ miles
Horse railway, 3ft 6in gauge, owned by Derby Canal.
OPD: 1795.   CSD: 1908.
REMS: Some of the route may be traced, especially in the vicinity of Little Eaton (364421).

LITTLE EATON–RIPLEY   6¾ miles
Midland Railway.
ACT: 22 July 1848.
OPD: 1 September 1856.
CSD: Passenger services into the old terminus: 2 June 1890; Branch passenger services: 1 June 1930 (excursions continued); Goods facilities at Old Yard (former terminus): 31 May 1954; Goods traffic over Denby–Ripley section: 1 April 1963; Denby goods facilities: 4 January 1965; South of Denby the line remains in use for colliery traffic.
REMS: *Denby*: station building (386472)*; *Ripley*: site of Old Yard—though no buildings remain (405496) (page 201).

ILKESTON TOWN BRANCH   ¾ mile
Midland Railway.
ACT: 4 August 1845.   OPD: 6 September 1847.
CSD: 2 May 1870; re-opened: 1 July 1879; finally closed: 16 June 1947 (Pass); 15 June 1959 (Gds); Ilkeston Junction: 2 January 1967.
REMS: *Ilkeston Town*: goods shed, platform, footbridge

(465425); Ilkeston Junction: branch platform (474426)
USES: Most of Ilkeston Town station site is occupied by a
Midland General bus garage.

BASFORD–BENNERLEY JUNCTION $5\frac{1}{4}$ miles
Midland Railway.
ACT: 25 July 1872.
OPD: Basford Junction–Watnall Colliery: 3 December 1877
(Coal); Throughout: 12 August 1879 (Gds); 1 September
1882 (Pass).
CSD: Passenger services: 1 January 1917; Goods facilities—
Kimberley: 1 January 1951, Watnall: 1 February 1954; Sid-
ings still exist at Bennerley Junction.
REMS: *Kimberley*: station buildings, goods shed (497449)*;
Watnall: 151yd tunnel, traces of platforms, abutments of col-
liery line overbridge—access from driveway in village (5045
53)*; *Awsworth*: embankment under GNR viaduct (484446).
USES: Watnall station site served as a wartime RAF station
which is now derelict. At Bulwell the trackbed has disappeared
beneath housing developments.

BUTTERLEY–LANGLEY MILL 6 miles
Midland Railway.
ACTS: Ripley–Butterley: 3 July 1884; Ripley–Heanor: 25
June 1886; Heanor–Langley Mill: 11 June 1891.
OPD: Butterley–Heanor: 2 June 1890 (Pass); Heanor–
Langley Mill: 1 October 1895 (Pass).
CSD: Passenger services—Langley Mill to Ripley (Marehay
Junction): 1 January 1917; Ripley to Butterley: 1 October
1917; Langley Mill to Butterley reopened: 3 May 1920; Lang-
ley Mill to Ripley (Marehay Junction) including Langley
Mill branch platform finally closed: 4 May 1926; Ripley to
Butterley: 1 June 1930; Langley Mill (Erewash Valley sta-
tion): 2 January 1967; Goods services—Heanor goods: 1
September 1951 (branch from Langley Mill); Ripley goods
(new station): 1 April 1963 (branch from Little Eaton direc-

tion); Line from Langley Mill to Bailey Brook Colliery existed until 1973.

REMS: *Langley Mill*: branch platforms—access from opposite side of main road to main station drive (449469)*; *Cross Hill & Codnor*: station building (419489)*; *Ripley*: road bridge over tracks at Marehay Junction (403492) (below), new station—platforms in cutting, booking office (402505)*.

USES: Cross Hill & Codnor station serves as a storebuilding for an engineering firm.

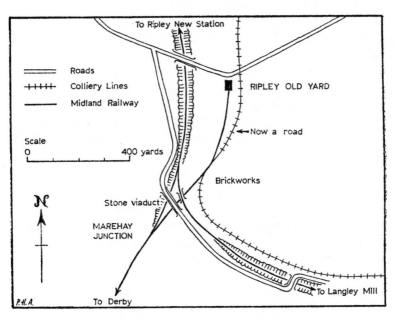

Plan of the railway system at Ripley

BASFORD–EGGINGTON JUNCTION 22¾ miles

Great Northern Railway.

ACT: 25 July 1872.

OPD: Basford–Awsworth Junction: September 1875 (Coal); 1 August 1876 (Pass)—in both cases associated with the Pinxton branch; Awsworth Junction–Eggington Junction: 1 April 1878.

CSD: Derby Friargate–Eggington Junction passenger services: 4 December 1939; Breadsall station: 6 April 1953; Derby Friargate–Basford North passenger services: 7 September 1964; Derby goods facilities: 4 September 1967; Colliery and iron ore traffic over line east of Derby: 6 May 1968; Ilkeston North goods facilities: 3 June 1968; Derby–Eggington Junction retained for freight and excursion trains until 3 February 1964 and is in use west of Mickleover for BR research.

REMS: *Basford*: viaduct across Leen valley (543440)*; *Kimberley*: station buildings (499448)*, limestone cutting and 268yd tunnel—can be reached from station (505451)*; *Ilkeston*: station buildings (463427)*, viaduct across Erewash valley (472438)*; *West Hallam*: station buildings (425408); *Breadsall*: station buildings (368394), viaduct (363383); *Derby*: bridge across Friargate, remains of station (346363)*, locomotive shed (337362); *Mickleover*: station buildings— probably the best preserved (307358)*; portal of 463yd tunnel —observe from road bridge; *Etwall*: station buildings (2643 16).

USES: Mickleover, West Hallam, Breadsall & Kimberley station houses are still occupied. Parts of Derby and Ilkeston stations are used by motor traders, as is the site of Basford station. Etwall station now belongs to an engineering firm and the forecourt of Eggington Junction station is taken up by a caravan dealer.

AWSWORTH JUNCTION–PINXTON   7¾ miles
Great Northern Railway.
ACT: 25 July 1872.
OPD: September 1875 (Gds); 1 August 1876 (Pass).
CSD: Passenger services: 7 January 1963; Goods facilities: 7 January 1963, except for Eastwood and Newthorpe: 2 November 1964. Colliery traffic from Eastwood: 16 May 1966.
REMS: *Awsworth*: viaduct across Giltbrook valley (485446)*; *Jacksdale*: station buildings incorporated in viaduct (4445 16)*.

USES: Jacksdale station is occupied by a poultry equipment firm.

LEEN VALLEY JUNCTION–ANNESLEY $7\frac{1}{4}$ miles
Great Northern Railway.
ACT: 6 August 1880.   OPD: 1 October 1882.
CSD: Linby station: 1 July 1916; Bulwell Forest station: 23 September 1929; Passenger services: 14 September 1931; Hucknall goods facilities: 3 May 1965; Bestwood Junction–Leen Valley Junction (through traffic): 4 April 1960; Colliery traffic over remainder: 27 May 1968.
REMS: *Bulwell*: station house (551454); *Bestwood*: station houses (549472); *Linby*: railway cottages (536504)*, station house (534508); *Newstead*: bridge across driveway to New-stead Abbey (524527)*.
USE: Leen Valley Junction site is occupied by houses.

STANTON JUNCTION–HEANOR $3\frac{3}{4}$ miles
Great Northern Railway.
ACTS: Stanton Junction–Shipley: 16 July 1885; Shipley–Heanor: 5 July 1887.
OPD: Stanton Junction–Nutbrook Colliery: June 1886 (Coal); Passenger services throughout: 1 July 1891; Goods traffic to Heanor: 1 January 1892.
CSD: Advertised passenger service withdrawn: 30 April 1928 (but continued unadvertised, Marlpool having closed perma-nently); Advertised service reinstated: 2 October 1939; finally withdrawn: 4 December 1939; Heanor goods yard: 7 Octo-ber 1963; Nutbrook sidings–Stanton Junction: 16 December 1963.
REMS: *Marlpool*: ornate station houses, footbridge, traces of island platform beneath undergrowth (443449)*.

ANNESLEY–BULWELL COMMON $6\frac{1}{2}$ miles
Great Central Railway.
ACT: 28 March 1893.
OPD: Coal trains to London, together with Annesley shed:

July 1898; Passenger services: 15 March 1899.
CSD: Bulwell Hall Halt: 5 May 1930; 'Dido' replaced by
Trent bus: 16 September 1956 (worked occasionally at later
dates); Local passenger services, Hucknall Central and Bul-
well Common stations, most goods facilities: 4 March 1963;
Through Bournemouth–York expresses (and completely): 5
September 1966.
REMS: *Bulwell*: viaduct across Leen Valley (544458)*.
SETTING: A fine impression of the Leen Valley may be
obtained from above the obscured portal of the MS & L tunnel
through Robin Hood's Hills (510545).

BETWEEN MANSFIELD AND CHESTERFIELD

EARLY RAILWAYS   Approx 10 miles
Several horse railways, most of them linking collieries, sand
pits, iron mines and glassworks with the Chesterfield Canal,
were constructed in the Brimington, Staveley, Renishaw and
Killamarsh areas during the early 1800s.

MANSFIELD–PINXTON   8 miles
Mansfield & Pinxton Railway. Horse tramways associated
with Cromford Canal.
ACT: 16 June 1817.   OPD: 13 April 1819 (Gds);
1832 (Pass). Absorbed by Midland Railway: 15 February
1848.
CSD: Rebuilt, with deviations, as locomotive-worked line;
9 October 1849—present Pye Bridge to Mansfield route.
REMS: *Pinxton*: Boat Inn—original terminus (452543);
Kirkby in Ashfield: Embankment in Grives Wood (497552);
Mansfield: King's Mill viaduct (519598)*.

SUMMIT COLLIERY (KIRKBY IN ASHFIELD)–
ANNESLEY COLLIERY AND KIRKBY WOODHOUSE
                                                   3 miles
Midland Railway.
OPD: Nottingham–Kirkby: 2 October 1848; Kirkby to

Mansfield (rebuilt from Mansfield & Pinxton Railway): 9 October 1849; From a point north of Kirkby Woodhouse to Kirkby station (deviation of M & P): 15 August 1892.

CSD: Nottingham–Worksop passenger service: 12 October 1964; Pye Bridge–Kirkby in Ashfield passenger service: 6 September 1965; Kirkby–Annesley: 6 May 1968; Summit Colliery–Kirkby Woodhouse: 4 April 1972; Part of abandoned GNR Leen Valley Extension relaid in conjunction with this operation (page 206).

REMS: Kirkby in Ashfield East station buildings (504561)*.

SETTING: The maze of abandoned lines may be observed from a new footbridge (499558).

ROLLESTON JUNCTION–MANSFIELD 14¾ miles
Midland Railway.

Rolleston Junction–Southwell: ACT: 16 July 1846; OPD: 1 July 1847; CSD: 1 August 1849; OPD: 12 April 1852; CSD: 14 March 1853; OPD: 1 September 1860; CSD: 15 June 1959; Gds: 1964.

Southwell–Mansfield:

ACT: 5 July 1865.   OPD: 3 April 1871.

CSD: Regular passenger services: 12 August 1929—through excursions and race specials continued; Goods services withdrawn by 1965; From Mansfield to Rainworth the track remains in use for colliery traffic.

REMS: *Southwell*: station house (706543)*, A612 road crossing house (710541)*—both dating from time of Mansfield extension; *Kirklington*: station buildings (675566); *Farnsfield*: station buildings (643573)*.

USES: Most station houses have been modernised and are still occupied.

WESTHOUSES–MANSFIELD WOODHOUSE 8¾ miles
Midland Railway.

ACTS: 7 June 1861; 28 July 1873; 30 July 1874.

OPD: Westhouses–Teversal: 1 May 1866; Teversal–Pleas-

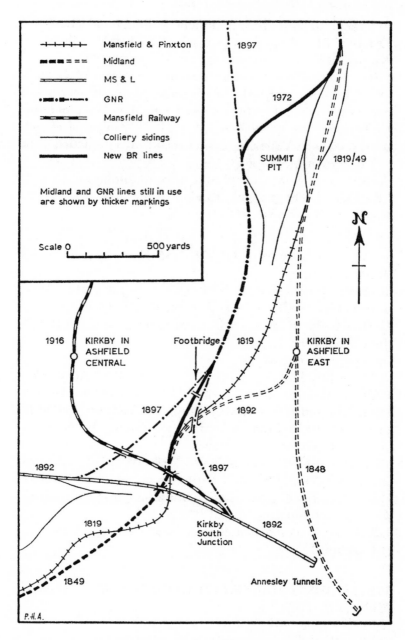

Legend:

━┼━┼━┼━	Mansfield & Pinxton
▬▬▬ ═ ═ ═	Midland
══════	MS & L
●▬●▬●▬	GNR
▬▬▬▬▬	Mansfield Railway
──────	Colliery sidings
▬▬▬▬	New BR lines

Midland and GNR lines still in use
are shown by thicker markings

Scale 0   500 yards

1897

1972

SUMMIT
PIT

1819/49

N

1916   KIRKBY IN   Footbridge   1819   KIRKBY IN
         ASHFIELD   ASHFIELD
         CENTRAL   EAST

         1897   1892

1892   1848

         1819   1897

                  Kirkby
                  South   1892
                  Junction

1849   Annesley Tunnels

P.H.A.

Plan of the railways at Kirkby in Ashfield

ley: 2 April 1877; Pleasley–Mansfield Woodhouse: 1 May 1886 (Colliery traffic); Passenger services throughout: 1 May 1886.

CSD: Whiteborough station: 4 October 1926; Regular passenger services: 28 July 1930; Most goods facilities by 1957; Line still open for colliery traffic as far east as Pleasley.
REMS: *Tibshelf*: only surviving station building (438598).
SETTING: Course of the line along the attractive Pleasley Vale is worth examining.

STAVELEY–PLEASLEY   8½ miles
Midland Railway.
ACTS: 21 July 1863; 29 June 1875; 16 July 1883.
OPD: In stages, culminating with Glapwell–Pleasley: 1 September 1890. (Colliery traffic); Passenger services throughout: 1 September 1890.
CSD: Regular passenger services: 28 July 1930; Most goods services withdrawn in LMS days, except Bolsover: 1962; Line still open for colliery traffic as far south as Bramley Vale.
REMS: *Glapwell*: station building (466663)*.
SETTING: Course of line past Rowthorne and Hardwick Hall is worth visiting.
USES: Glapwell station building is a meeting place for the Full Revival Gospel Mission.

SUTTON JUNCTION–SUTTON IN ASHFIELD   ¾ mile
Midland Railway.
ACT: 25 July 1890.   OPD: 1 May 1893.
CSD: Passenger service withdrawn: 1 January 1917; Reinstated: 9 July 1923; Withdrawn again: 4 May 1926; Reinstated: 20 September 1926; Finally withdrawn: 26 September 1949; Unadvertised workmen's service and freight facilities withdrawn: 1 October 1951; Sutton Junction: 12 October 1964 (Pass).
REMS: Tunnel under branch dating from construction of Mansfield Railway (502584).

BEIGHTON–ANNESLEY $23\frac{3}{4}$ miles
Manchester, Sheffield & Lincolnshire Railway.
ACT: 26 July 1889.
OPD: Beighton–Staveley: 1 December 1891 (Gds); 1 June 1892 (Pass); Staveley–Annesley: 24 October 1892 (Gds); 2 January 1893 (Passenger service through to Nottingham London Road).
CSD: Pilsley station: 2 November 1959; Local passenger services: 4 March 1963; Most goods facilities by 1965; Through passenger trains: 5 September 1966; Rails were retained for colliery access but are now cut back to Duckmanton Junction.
REMS: *Duckmanton*: junctions with LDECR (425708); *Kirkby in Ashfield*: South Junction—with GNR & Mansfield Railway (500552).
USES: An unusually large proportion of the trackbed has disappeared under landscape improvement schemes—notably at Tibshelf (439608), Pilsley (430624) and Kirkby in Ashfield (505549). Only the formation and certain bridges remain elsewhere.

CHESTERFIELD LOOP $9\frac{1}{4}$ miles
Manchester, Sheffield & Lincolnshire Railway.
ACTS: Staveley–Chesterfield: 26 July 1889; Chesterfield–Heath: 25 July 1890.
OPD: Staveley–Staveley Works: 1 December 1891 (Gds); Staveley–Chesterfield: 4 June 1892; Chesterfield–Heath; 3 July 1893.
CSD: Grassmoor station: 28 October 1940; Brimington station: 2 January 1956; All passenger services: 4 March 1963; All traffic south of Chesterfield: 1963; Chesterfield goods facilities: 11 September 1967; Staveley Works traffic subsequently diverted on to Midland.
REMS: *Chesterfield*: 445yd tunnel—note different profiles of north and south portals and outsized smoke vent (386710)*; *Brimington*: station building (392737)*.
SETTING: The intensely industrialised surroundings of the

loop are well seen at Temple Normanton (415680) and Staveley Works (416746).
USES: 1½ miles of trackbed at the southern end has been used for a new section of A617 Mansfield–Chesterfield road. Brimington station is used by a car undersealing business.

CHESTERFIELD–LANGWITH JUNCTION   10 miles
Lancashire, Derbyshire & East Coast Railway.
ACT: 8 July 1891.   OPD: 8 March 1897.
Absorbed by Great Central Railway on 1 January 1907, during which year the junctions at Duckmanton were opened (433708).
CSD: Passenger services: 3 December 1951; Shirebrook North (Langwith Junction until 1924) remained open for Lincoln service until 19 September 1955 and for seasonal Skegness trains until 5 September 1964; Goods facilities withdrawn from Chesterfield Market Place in 1957 (access via Duckmanton Junctions) and Shirebrook North in 1965.
REMS: *Chesterfield*: Market Place station building and concourse (380711)*, remains of viaduct (387705)* *Scarcliffe*: eastern portal of 2624yd Bolsover tunnel and exceptionally deep approach cutting—access from footpath in centre of village (495686)*, station house (500685); *Langwith Junction*: main station buildings, platforms, footbridge (526687)*.
SETTING: A splendid impression of the approach to Chesterfield may be obtained from the embankment high above the Rother valley (388705).
USES: Chesterfield station is a carpet warehouse. A large section of the route through Chesterfield has been obliterated by land reclamation and road schemes.

LANGWITH JUNCTION–BEIGHTON   12½ miles
Lancashire, Derbyshire & East Coast Railway.
ACT: 8 July 1891.
OPD: Langwith Junction–Barlborough: 16 November 1896 (Colliery traffic); Goods services throughout, Langwith Junction–Clowne passenger service: 8 March 1897; Passenger

service extended to Sheffield Midland: 30 May 1900. LDECR absorbed by GCR in 1907.

CSD: Upperthorpe & Killamarsh station: 7 July 1930; Local passenger services: 10 September 1939; Closed completely: 9 January 1967; Excursions and freight continued until late 1960s. The track is used for colliery traffic as far south as Westhorpe. For two miles north of Langwith Junction the branch serves as a link with the Midland system.

REMS: *Spinkhill*: station building and western portal of 501yd tunnel (457791); *Clowne*: passenger station buildings, goods shed, station house (494757)*.

USES: Spinkhill station is a house. The booking office at Clowne has been converted into a bank.

KIRKBY IN ASHFIELD–LANGWITH JUNCTION
9¾ miles

Great Northern Railway.

ACT: 20 June 1892.

OPD: Kirkby South Junction–Silverhill Colliery: 9 February 1897 (Coal); Annesley–Skegby passenger service: 4 April 1898; Pleasley–Shirebrook Colliery: 26 November 1900 (Coal); Skegby–Shirebrook South passenger service: 1 November 1901; GNR passenger trains extended to Langwith Junction after GCR took over LDECR.

CSD: Kirkby north to west curve disused by 1918, removed by 1922; Local passenger services: 14 September 1931; Sutton in Ashfield Town reopened: 20 February 1956; Nottingham service withdrawn again: 17 September 1956; Excursions and freight traffic continued into 1960s; Closed completely: 27 May 1968.

REMS: *Sutton in Ashfield*: cutting, bridges, goods buildings (496592); *Skegby*: passenger station (495611)*; *Teversal*: passenger station, house (478616)*; *Shirebrook*: rock cutting —observe from overbridge (519666) or from site of station, where the house still exists (522673)*, embankment through town (526679)*.

USES: Skegby station is used as offices by an engineering firm.

KIKBY IN ASHFIELD–CLIPSTONE

11 miles

Mansfield Railway. Worked by GCR from outset.

ACT: 26 July 1910.

OPD: Clipstone–Mansfield Colliery (Coal): 13 June 1913; Mansfield Colliery–Mansfield (Gds): 2 June 1914; Mansfield –Kirkby South Junction (Gds): 4 September 1916; Passenger services: 2 April 1917. Absorbed by LNER: 1 January 1923.

CSD: Local passenger services: 2 January 1956; Excursion traffic continued; Mansfield goods facilities: 13 June 1966 (a BR warehouse until 1972); The line north of Mansfield Colliery remains in use.

REMS: *Sutton in Ashfield*: station building, cutting (5045 86)*; *Mansfield*: goods yard buildings (540603).

SETTING: An interesting section of route is that which crosses the mill dam of the 'duckpond' (533597).

USES: An unusually large part of this line is being obscured beyond recognition: at Kirkby in Ashfield the long cutting is being filled with colliery waste; almost the entire course of the railway through Mansfield is being redeveloped. A 'Cash & Carry' warehouse occupies the cutting south of Mansfield (527597). Sutton station and goods yard are used by an engineering firm.

Corrections to 1 June 1973

Chesterfield Market Place station demolished in April 1973. Mansfield Central station and goods shed cleared during 1973. Work has started on the link for gypsum traffic at Loughborough.

Bibliography

The following list of books and articles is by no means exhaustive but serves as a guide to the most informative literature concerning the railway companies and individual routes described in these pages. Certain publications contain their own bibliographies, and for those eager to examine a specific subject in greater detail these are denoted by an asterisk. Works giving background information or general accounts appear first, followed by an outline of source material for each chapter in turn where entries are arranged to coincide with the pattern of topics dealt with in the relevant region. Certain volumes are mentioned more than once with the intention of directing readers to the appropriate chapter or volume in a far-reaching survey. Finally, abbreviations are employed as follows:

Derbyshire Countryside = *DC*
Locomotive Journal = *LJ*
Leicester Museum Collection = *LM*
Railway Magazine = *RM*
Railway World = *RW*
Railways = *RYS*
Trains Illustrated = *TI*
Transactions of the Leics. Archaeological & Historical Socy. = *TLAS*

BACKGROUND BOOKS

W. J. Gorden. *Our Home Railways*, two volumes (reprinted). A lively account of the four major companies represented in the East Midlands is contained here

H. C. Casserley & C. C. Dorman. *Railway History in Pictures —The Midlands* (Newton Abbot, 1969). Includes illustrations of several closed East Midland lines

E. G. Barnes. *Rise of the Midland Railway* (1966)

C. Hamilton-Ellis. *The Midland Railway* (1953)

F. S. Williams. *The Midland Railway—Its Rise & Progress* (1876, reprinted Newton Abbot, 1968)

Charles H. Grinling. *The History of the Great Northern Railway* (1898, reprinted, 1966). The standard work on this company; contains plenty of information on East Midland lines

George Dow. *Great Central* (Vol 1—1959; Vol 2—1962; Vol 3—1965). A full and excellent account of all railways associated with this company in the area

W. L. Steel. *The History of the London and North Western Railway* (1914)

B. Baxter. *Stone Blocks and Iron Rails—Tramroads* (Newton Abbot, 1966)*. Contains a wealth of information on early railways in the East Midlands

David Smith. *The Industrial Archaeology of the East Midlands* (Newton Abbot, 1965)

C. R. Clinker & J. M. Firth. *Register of Closed Passenger Stations and Goods Depots 1830–1970* (Padstow)

HIGH LEICESTERSHIRE

C. E. Lee. 'The Belvoir Castle Railway' (*RM*, June 1938)

P. H. V. Banyard. 'Skegness is so bracing' (*Leicester Railway Society Review*, 1968). An amusing account of excursion traffic from Belgrave Road

P. H. V. Banyard & C. P. Walker. 'The Leicester Belgrave Road branch lives another year' (*TI*, July 1961)

H. L. Hopwood. 'The GN & LNW Joint Railway' (*RM*, June 1918)

C. P. Walker. 'The GN & LNW Joint line through Leicestershire' (*RW*, September & October 1963)

E. Tonks. *The Ironstone Railways and Tramways of the Midlands* (1959), Chapter 10

WEST OF LEICESTER

R. Abbott. 'The Railways of the Leicester Navigation Company' (*TLAS*, Vol XXXI—1955). A very fine account

C. R. Clinker & C. Hadfield. 'The Ashby de la Zouch Canal and Its Railways' (*TLAS*, Vol XXXIV—1958)

C. E. Lee. 'Swannington: One Time Railway Centre' (*RM*, July 1939)

C. R. Clinker & G. Biddle. 'Swannington and Ticknall Today' (*RM*, April 1952)

C. R. Clinker. 'The Leicester and Swannington Railway' (*TLAS*, Vol XXX—1954). Includes everything worth knowing about the early years of this railway

C. R. Clinker. 'New Light on the Leicester and Swannington Railway' (*RM*, March 1953)

R. C. Riley. 'The Leicester West Bridge Branch' (*RW*, November 1963)

C. Stretton. 'The Ashby & Nuneaton Joint Railway' (*LM*)

W. A. Camwell. 'Some Railway Byways on the Leicestershire Border' (*RYS*, May 1952)

'The Burton and Ashby Light Railway' (*RM*, July 1906)

R. B. Parr. *An English Country Tramway* (Crich, 1970)

BETWEEN SYSTON AND PETERBOROUGH

C. Stretton. 'A History of the Syston & Peterborough Line' (*LJ*, December 1904)

R. H. Clark. *A Short History of the Midland & Great Northern Joint Railway* (Norwich, 1967)

A. J. Wrottesley. *The Midland & Great Northern Joint Railway* (Newton Abbot, 1970)

'The Stamford & Essendine Railway' (*RM*, September 1906)

D. L. Franks. *The Stamford & Essendine Railway* (Leeds, 1971)

E. Tonks. *The Ironstone Railways and Tramways of the Midlands* (1959), Chapter 9

CENTRAL LEICESTERSHIRE

George Dow. *Great Central* (Vols 2 & 3). A full account of the political background, construction and working of the London Extension

Leicester Museums. *The Last Main Line* (Leicester, 1968). Photographs from the Newton Collection of Leicester Museums

L. T. C. Rolt. *The Making of a Railway* (1971). A more extensive selection from the Newton Collection

HIGH DERBYSHIRE

C. P. Nicholson & P. Barnes. *Railways in the Peak District* (Clapham, Yorkshire, 1971). A good general survey

J. A. Patmore & J. Clarke. *Railway History in Pictures: North-West England* (Newton Abbot, 1968). Contains photographs of the Cromford & High Peak line

A. Rimmer. *The Cromford & High Peak Railway* (Lingfield, 1971)*. A comprehensive survey

D. S. Barrie & J. R. Hollick. 'The Cromford & High Peak Railway' (*RM*, November 1934)

J. F. Rhodes. 'The Cromford & High Peak Line' (*RW*, March 1967)

R. Christian. 'Ashbourne's Railway' (*DC*, Vol 20—1954)

K. P. Plant. *The Ashover Light Railway* (Lingfield, 1965)*. An extremely thorough account

'The Ashover Light Railway' (*RM*, October 1925)

'The Ashover Light Railway' (*RM*, September 1950)

CITY OF NOTTINGHAM

J. A. B. Hamilton. 'The Railways of Nottingham' (*RM*, February & March 1932). Describes all lines and their traffic in some detail

Railway Correspondence and Travel Society. *The Railways of Nottingham: Exhibition Programme* (Nottingham,

1969). A very colourful description of all Nottingham's railways

H. L. Hopwood. 'The Nottingham & Grantham Railway' (*RM*, May 1922)

J. P. Wilson. 'The Grantham–Nottingham Line' (*TI*, November 1956)

J. Marshall. 'The Nottingham Suburban Railway' (*RM*, June 1961). A very thorough piece of research

J. F. Gairns. 'Notable Railway Stations and their Traffic— Nottingham Victoria, LNER' (*RM*, September 1926)

R. Iliffe & W. Baguley. *Victorian Nottingham—Volume 5— Victoria Station and Its Approaches* (Nottingham, 1971). An excellent collection of old photographs illustrating the changes brought about by the Great Central line

NORTH AND WEST OF NOTTINGHAM

The Midland Railway Project Group. *The Railways of Derbyshire: Exhibition Programme* (Derby, 1971)

'Some unusual Routes of the Midland Railway' (*RYS*, December 1951)

Charles H. Grinling. *The History of the Great Northern Railway*, Chapters 16 to 19. A detailed analysis of the Derbyshire Extension lines

P. Stevenson. *The Nutbrook Canal: Derbyshire* (Newton Abbot, 1970)

J. Cupit. 'All stations to Pinxton' (*TI*, August 1955)

George Dow. *Great Central*, Volume 2. Contains further information on the northernmost part of the London Extension

BETWEEN MANSFIELD AND CHESTERFIELD

J. A. Birks & P. Coxon. 'The Mansfield & Pinxton Railway' (*RM*, July/August 1949—one issue)

J. Cupit. 'Snapshot of the Southwell Branch' (*TI*, June 1958)

Charles H. Grinling. *The History of the Great Northern Railway*, Chapters 24 and 25. An account of the Leen Valley Extension

George Dow. *Great Central*, Volume 2. History of the Derbyshire lines of the MS & L.

J. Cupit. 'The Lancashire, Derbyshire and East Coast Railway (*TI*, September & October 1956)

J. Cupit & W. Taylor. *The Lancashire, Derbyshire and East
Coast Railway* (Lingfield, 1966). A thorough survey

J. Francis. 'The Mansfield Railway' (*RM*, September 1915)

J. Cupit. 'The Mansfield Railway' (*TI*, February 1956)

Acknowledgements

Above all, I must thank Percy Banyard: without his help I could never have done justice to the railways described in this book. In 1898 his father moved from Guide Bridge to Leicester Central where he became a station inspector. Percy himself started in the locomotive department as a cleaner in 1917, became a fireman and then a driver on the Great Central line, and was made a motive power inspector at Colwick in 1950. Before his retirement in 1968 he became very well acquainted with most of the former Great Central and Great Northern routes in the East Midlands. But besides having an intricate knowledge of railway matters, Percy appreciated the humorous side of the job and developed a marvellous philosophy of life. Many of the local incidents and stories described in these pages emanate from his experiences. I value his friendship tremendously and offer him my deepest gratitude: my debt to him I cannot repay.

I would like to acknowledge the assistance given by the librarians at Nottingham, Mansfield and Chesterfield, Mrs F. Waters at Leicester Museum, the staff of the BRB Archives (now the Public Records Office), whose patience I sorely tried in tracing various Acts of Parliament, and Messrs C. R. Clinker & J. M. Firth whose *Register of Closed Passenger Stations and Goods Depots* proved an invaluable source of

ACKNOWLEDGEMENTS

information. Especial thanks are due to all those people who willingly went to so much trouble to locate, print and despatch the photographs reproduced.

I am also grateful to the following: Mr E. Tonks, Mr M. Billingham whose talk to the Leicester Railway Society in 1971 gave me valuable information on the Cliffe Hill Railway; Mr J. Cupit of Nottingham; Mr F. Pike of Kimberley East Stationhouse; Messrs Widdowson and Clow who live in railway cottages at Barnstone and Great Dalby respectively; and finally the many retired railwaymen and colliers, the regulars at the Railway Inn at Whiteborough for example, whose tales and anecdotes told over a pint of good Nottinghamshire ale gave me a great deal of inspiration. I think a tribute is also due to the enterprising engineers and architects who laid the railway system across the three counties and to the resourceful men who have enabled it to serve the needs of industry and local communities for well over a century.

A special word of thanks is due to Mrs Joan Baker of Kineton who typed, checked and corrected the script without a word of complaint. In fact, to everyone who gave assistance while I was undertaking work for this book I offer my grateful thanks: I only hope that you feel your efforts have been worthwhile.

Index

Page numbers in italics indicate an illustration